THE FELINE MYSTIQUE

ALSO BY CLEA SIMON

Fatherless Women:
How We Change After We Lose Our Dads

Mad House:
Growing Up in the Shadows of Mentally Ill Siblings

ON THE MYSTERIOUS

CONNECTION BETWEEN

WOMEN AND CATS

THE
FELINE
MYSTIQUE

Clea Simon

ST. MARTIN'S PRESS ❧ NEW YORK

www.stmartins.com

Design by Kathryn Parise

ISBN 0-312-26881-5

10   9   8   7   6   5   4   3

In memory of Cyrus T. Cat,
our eminence grisé

Contents

Preface		xiii
1.	A Cat of One's Own	1
2.	Bonding	28
3.	Household Gods	49
4.	When the Fur Flew	71
5.	The Sensual Kitty	86
6.	Meows and Whispers	103
7.	Obsession	123
8.	Littering	142
9.	The Wild Side	161
10.	Letting Go	192
11.	The Solace of Cats	214
	Acknowledgments	230
	Cat Rescue Organizations	233
	Bibliography	235

Preface

This is a love story. This is a love story between a woman and a cat, between women and cats, between all women and all cats. This is a love story that has lasted through history, since before history, and this is a love story that is being played out as you read this. This is a love story that cannot last. But this is a love story that renews itself and begins again, full of life and joy and promise, because this is a love story that will never end. This is a love story that has no beginning and no end. This is a love story.

My chapter in this love story began seventeen years ago, when I first met a small gray kitten. Not yet old enough to leave his mother, this small gray kitten would grow to be the companion of my single adult years, the sole emotional support of my post-college life as I built a career, found friends, and finally met and married a kind and decent man. Our part of this story ends, as all lives end, with gradual weakness and decline, with tears and denial, and finally heartbreakingly as such friendships must, with love and kindness and with promises kept. This is a story of myself and my cat, and by extension of all women and all cats, and it is a story that has already begun anew. This is a love story for all of us, for this is our story, about the bonds we forge and the unspoken connections that hold us together in warmth, in affection, in loyalty, and in sympathy, us and our feline companions, complements to each other's natures, fellow creatures. This is a love story. This is our story.

THE FELINE

MYSTIQUE

1

A CAT OF ONE'S OWN

"Will I ever find someone to love?" I remember asking my therapist that about ten years ago, not for the first time and not for the last. "Will I ever be able to sustain a relationship, I mean one with someone other than my parents, for more than six months at a time?" For whatever reason that week, I was feeling particularly desperate.

"You already have," my shrink, a petite woman packed full of wisdom, told me. "I've seen you, learning and growing together. Allowing your lives to come together." I waited, wondering who I had forgotten. "But for better or worse, this relationship is with your cat."

I remember feeling a little peeved with her answer. Wasn't she taking me seriously? But then I flashed back to a few years earlier. My then-roommate Susan had come home to find me, as usual, seated by the window, cuddling Cyrus, the gray mixed-breed longhair I'd adopted the year before.

"He really is beautiful," said Susan, a big, smart woman with a big, smart grin. "He's clean and elegant, sensitive to your moods, and, in his own way, he is utterly devoted to you." I was, of course, the one who fed him, I thought, but I didn't want to interrupt.

"He's got the long hair you like, and the brilliant green eyes." She let her phrases casually roll. "He's got that smooth way of walking down the hall. One of these days, you're going to pick him up and kiss him. And he's going to turn into a handsome man, with the same beautiful hair and the same striking eyes. And for once he'll be able to take you in his arms and embrace you right back.

"And then he's going to say to you, 'Aren't you sorry you had me fixed?' "

At this point Cyrus squirmed to be let loose, and Susan, flashing that big easy smile, followed him out of the room. In the years that have followed, I have wondered if my roommate knew how much her good-natured ribbing touched on the truth. I have since married a terrific man, a cat lover like myself. And in some crucial characteristics—the loyalty paired with a sense of self, the healthy pride, the green eyes, though not, I must note, the surgery—he does resemble the cat who now shares both our lives. Her lighthearted prediction came true, after a fashion, and Susan and I had a good laugh over this when she came East for my wedding. But since then I have had reason to question the apparent coincidences my deceptively easygoing roommate pointed out. For although these memories make me smile, she's sharp enough to have alerted me to their more serious shading as well, bringing me back as good friends will to some basic lessons about the nature of love and growth, of what I need for myself and what I can—or want to—share of my life, that I first learned and that I continue to explore through my relationship with my cat.

It can seem strange, at first, to think in such profound terms about this most domestic of relationships. But if we allow ourselves to consider it seriously, we will see that there is great power and great potential here, built up in the closeness of our bond and the special understanding that can exist between female human and feline. A sympathy exists between us, a sense of common cause between the petting and the purr that allows us to grow and dream, that allows us, the human half of the equation, to draw upon previously untapped parts of ourselves.

Consider, for a start, just how easy it is to make light of this relationship in any of its stages: the lonely single woman who sees her cat as her mistress, her lover, or her boss is the stuff of endless jokes and urban legends. As is the depressed wife who confides in her cat, rather than her husband, or the "crazy old cat lady" who collects felines like her peers collect porcelain knickknacks. Cat and woman, bound to each other and often separated in some essential way from the world, this pairing has provided material for myriad parodies. As long ago as 1801 playwright George Colman used the name Lucretia McTab in his comedy *The Poor Gentleman* to signal to readers that this character, a confirmed spinster, was tabby-cat like, a stereotypical cat woman. To fulfill the caricature, he made her foolishly proud, so deluded about her own worth that she snubs her benefactors because they are of lesser blood. She was followed in the British popular press by *Old Dame Trot and her Comical Cat* in 1806 and *Dame Wiggins of Lee* in 1823 who cohabited with "seven fine cats," both early cartoons that won their laughs at the expense of similarly single cat-loving women of a certain age, and there are many who accept these characteristics—the pride, the aloofness, the antimale bias—about all of us cat women and look no further.

The basis for the easy humor, the stereotypes that serve as

fodder for office jokes and TV sitcoms, lies in our recognition of a type. We can all envision the classic "witch," a hag with a scary cat. We have also grown accustomed to its contemporary equivalent, caricatured in Nicole Hollander's cartoon "Sylvia": the neurotic thirtysomething who pampers her pet because she lacks a man or a baby. These stereotypes live on because they are so immediately recognizable, they've become a form of social shorthand to signify maladjusted women. But these simplistic images acknowledge a larger truth. In their negative way, the proliferation of such images serves as evidence of the connection between feline and female.

The language of metaphor reveals the depth of the bond. Think of cats and how they are described: as sleek and graceful, to use some of the more positive words. Slinky or fluid or poised. Or as duplicitous and sly, by those who dislike them. But always, essentially, in terms ordinarily reserved for feminine attributes. And think of the colloquial language used to describe women, whether we are catty or kittenish, "cat fighting" when we turn on each other, or "catting around" when we play the field. Whether we be idealized into the sexy nighttime prowler who is Catwoman or dismissed as simply "pussy," women and cats are so closely identified as to be, in our descriptive language at least, almost interchangeable, particularly when either of us retreat behind our essential personal mysteries. We are feline; we epitomize sensuality. We radiate cool: "Two tricks over the years have taught me how to conceal my tears," wrote Colette, the most feline of French authors. "That of hiding my thoughts, and that of darkening my mascara." Compare that enigmatic, elegant image to the kohl-rimmed eyes of the calmly staring tabby, and remember that the cat is the basis for the riddling sphinx. Cats—to the rest of the world at any rate—embody both our worst and our best traits.

We have become linked in the world's eyes, elevated to contemporary icons: The young girl who learns to care for, and be gentle with, her kitten. The working woman who relaxes when she drops her briefcase and bulging purse to place her hand, instead, on her pet's soft, warm fur. And the older woman, too often alone, for whom the quiet cat on the windowsill is a more generous companion than her memories. Reaching beyond the more simple, laughable stereotypes, these pairings represent different facets of the real connection between each person and her pet. We see such relationships repeated throughout our lives; we may find ourselves in first one and then another, much as we model ourselves on different archetypes—daughter or mother, career powerhouse or crone—at various times. Even if we do not fulfill all these roles, even as we leave those we've outgrown behind, we sense the rightness of such iconic images, the bond between a woman and her feline companion.

We don't mean to snub dogs and their people. Clearly, dog owners also experience what they believe is an honest and true emotional bond. But the quality of the connection seems to be essentially different: Dog owners (who still edge out cat owners as a group, although the total number of pet kitties beat pooches more than a decade ago) report their relish in becoming physically involved in their pets' active lives, walking and running and romping with them; in surveys, dog owners overwhelmingly respond that they feel closest to their pets while playing or exercising with them. Their bonding comes primarily through sweat and motion. We cat owners, and there are more than 35 million of us in the United States, split our responses among more domestic pastimes; according to the American Animal Hospital

Association, we report that we bond most closely either while sleeping with our pets or while stroking or grooming them.

The nature of our connection adds to our mystique, to the element of unknown that confuses so many outside observers of our relationship. It's a different kind of tie than the classic bond that linked Timmy to his Lassie, and it works particularly well with the strengths that we, as women, have been encouraged to develop in communication, cooperation, and understanding. As is so often true with dog people versus cat people, the major difference can be seen as a pitting of extroversion against introversion, of activity, if you will, versus intimacy.

The truth, of course, grows not only from which animal we prefer but from how we choose to relate. I know of one woman, for example, who cuddles her dachshunds as if she were nursing them, unfolding all her secrets into their dark velvet ears. She is the exception, however, and if we are to look at the pet-owning population as a whole, the paradigm becomes clear. Dog people, on the whole, seem to enjoy being taken out of their lives by their pets; we cat owners, and we do include an increasing number of men in our midst, instead welcome our pets *into* the emotional fabric of our lives. In many ways, we use our cats as mediums into ourselves, seeing, in how we view our cats, who we are, and discovering, in how we treat them, what handling we think we deserve from the world. Both types of bonding have their value, but we who have become cat people treasure the quiet and personal nature of our relationship, the steady purr over the joyful bark. It is, like so many things female (and perhaps, like so many things undervalued in our go-go competitive world), a subtler treasure. And in this quiet, private space we find our courage and spirit, we find new value in our feminine nature, we find the strengths that we may have misperceived as weaknesses. In short, as we uncover the layers of this connection—the bond between the female and the feline—we find real jewels, core truths from which we can all learn.

When I first got my cat, I had no idea of the adventure on which I was embarking. I was about to turn twenty-three, and as confused and lonely as any of us are at that age, when I met Cyrus, who was to become my first true cat. Yes, I had grown up with felines. There had been James, whom my brother had brought home from college during a break and left with us. I had seen that black-and-white kitten grow into the terror tom of the neighborhood, bringing in squirrels and birds and fathering half the town's litters. And when he failed to return after one wild summer storm, he had been followed by the dumb, sweet, and ultimately shortlived Thomas; and then Tara. But these had been household cats, co-siblings, as it were, to accompany my growing up, the kind of cats who went to the vet only to be neutered, or when scrapes with the neighbors' pets resulted in particularly persistent infections or particularly ugly cuts. None of them received the care and loving that would distinguish my pet. None of them reached the lonely places within me. None of them was personally or specifically speaking, *my* cat.

Cyrus, however, was my cat from the moment I saw him, just a few weeks old, clumsy and squeaking in a friend's basement apartment. With a tail still stiff and pointed, and a tiny bat face defined by huge gray ears, he was an unprepossessing little beast, the runt of the litter. I don't remember what I was thinking that day when I dropped by to visit my friend and her cats. My friend was a bartender and, like myself, she lived for the club scene, so we didn't often meet in the light of day. But I recall the afternoon sun streaking through the one high-set window as I leaned over the cluster of kittens in their cardboard nest and watched as my shadow caused the young siblings to scatter. Cyrus, the runt, tried to follow suit, but ended up sitting on his fuzzy butt. I picked him up; he fit into the palm of my hand.

Then that defiant pink mouth opened to mew silently up at me and—boom!—I became a statistic: I, along with 34 percent of the population (to quote the Pet Food Institute's 2000 figures), had fallen for a cat, one of more than 73 million now living as pets in this country. And although most pets of all kinds are still owned by families, I was a member of the vast majority of single cat owners: a woman who had chosen, or been chosen by, a cat. (The 2000–2001 American Pet Products Manufacturers Association Pet Owners Survey reports that 13 percent of all cats are owned by women living alone; suggestively, 85 percent of the cat owners who responded to their questions were women.)

Although I didn't understand the complex factors that went into our finding each other, I felt the click. This assertive little animal had triggered some response in me. It would be too easy to say he activated some latent maternal instinct, that his helplessness brought out the nurturing woman in my punk-rock loving breast. Yes, my loneliness and my readiness to grow came into play, and I did learn to nurture that kitten. But even more so, that diminutive creature served as a stand-in for some of my then more inchoate dreams for what I wanted in life and for whom I would become.

In some sense, I fit the iconic image of the lost girl who finds a kitten to love. I was also an adult, albeit a young and somewhat wayward one, and at some level, by choosing that kitten I was granting myself a new level of freedom and responsibility, acknowledging that I could expand my life from what it was then. Although I was trying to make a name for myself as a music critic, and thought of myself as a denizen of the night most naturally attired in black leather, some small, ignored part of me also saw myself in that kitten. By taking it to my heart, I was acknowledging that there were other facets to my personality; that despite my fierce independence, I too had a right to nurturing attention. That despite my allegiance to the "scene," as we called it, I could have something positive in my days as well. That despite the haphazard start of my glorious career, half underpaid freelance and half secretarial schlock work, I could allow myself to begin to imagine a future. I could handle the responsibility, the cans and litterboxes, and accept the love. By adopting a kitten, I was deciding that I, too, was worth the investment.

Of course, I knew none of this then. All I knew at that point was that I was ready to have a cat, to care for a cat, and more than ready to let myself be loved by so singular a pet. Whether I chose Cyrus or he chose me, or whether any other kitten would have stolen my heart had this particular gray one not appeared, I didn't know. Nor did I care. When I wasn't hanging out at the Rat, my favorite club, I wanted to be home with my cat. My heart had cried out to this tiny long-haired kitten, and his imperious bat face had answered. The connection was made.

Within a few years, I had progressed from my postcollege roommate situation into my own rent-controlled apartment. And also, conveniently, into another role. No longer quite so unsure of myself nor so uniformly clad in black, I was dating a variety of men, many of whom Cyrus reacted to for good or for ill with an amazingly wide range of, shall we say, biological responses. And I had built up a coterie of close female friends, many of whom also had cats. I was beginning to write about life outside of clubland, as well; an activity that helped me understand who I was and what I wanted out of my budding life, and I often found myself aided in this otherwise solitary (and frequently frustrating) activity by the now mature cat who liked to

curl up on the chair next to mine as I pecked away at the key-
board. I was settling into my young adulthood. I was living
alone, except, of course, for Cyrus, and despite the richness that
existed in my life—and in the lives of my friends—I found I was
perpetuating another stereotype. I was a single, urban woman,
with a single, urban cat.

The stories about those of us who could be described this way
are legion, and with reason. First, we're a marketing professional's dream. Cats are the most rapidly growing population of
pets in this country, up 3.4 percent from 1999 to 2000 (according to the pet-food group), having passed dogs somewhere in the
mid-eighties thanks to the increase in multiple-cat ownership.
Women who live only with cats make up one of the fastest-
growing groups of cat owners, responsible for a large chunk of
the nearly $750 million we spend each year on food, care, and
treats. Women are now the majority of vets as well, according to
the American Animal Hospital Association. There are millions
of us, many of us cohabiting with more than one feline at any
given time, and many of us living with only our cat companions.

This is not only the relationship in its purest form, it is also its
most frequently ridiculed one. Take, for example, the urban
myth of the elderly woman who lives with only her cats. As the
myth is told and retold, it always centers on a basic storyline. In
it, the woman foolishly shuns human contact and dies a recluse.
Because of her dearth of human connections, her death is not
discovered for quite some time. When her body is found, it has
been mauled or eaten by her feline companions.

Leslie has heard this story bandied about, and when she's
being candid she'll admit it worries her. A Manhattan lawyer
with a sharp wit and sometimes sharper mouth, the thirtysomething brunette and her two cats have lived alone for quite a few
years. Sometimes, she says, she wonders if anyone else could

ever fit into their tight union, a conspiracy of three coexisting in a two-room downtown co-op. "I often say to my friends, 'I'm turning into one of those crazy ladies with her cats.' They all know what I mean, because they're exactly the same way." She laughs and points out that all her single city friends also have the requisite Rollerblades that now complete the stereotype, as well as the national average 2.1 cats, but her laughter has an edge to it. She's heard the story too often, and each time it haunts her.

What we're hearing is her nervousness and her reaction, as she tries to shrug it off. Beneath those nerves and that tough shell, however, is something that all of us who consider ourselves cat women need to be wary of. Leslie is afraid for a reason, and making light of her anxiety is part of her defense. Many of us laugh in such a way at such stories, at least among ourselves. By doing so we put ourselves down—just a bit—to anticipate and save ourselves from the scorn of others. We distance ourselves and repeat the stories as a sort of reality check about what the world outside our cozy union is like. Because this perennially recurring story, in all its forms, is designed to serve as a cautionary tale to uppity women.

On the surface, it's simple: the tale reprimands women who live only with pets and warns us against becoming like the old lady, against seemingly choosing cats over people. This is a tale we can laugh at, a fate we can dismiss. Leslie, for example, would prefer to have a human companion as well as her two felines; she often talks about wanting children, as do many of her friends. Her situation—living with only her cats—will, she hopes, be temporary. But even as we chuckle, the story sinks its barbs in. It makes us nervous about who we are, for it warns us against building ourselves into the kind of women—aggressive, independent, smart—whom human companions, notably men, will not want. It warns us to reconsider before it is too late. Its moral, even at this level, is not subtle: "A human could care for you, but a cat, well, a cat will just use you whether you live or die. Don't be so sure you can make it on your own." Our desire for personal and professional fulfillment is set up as antagonistic to our very survival. Our cats mutate from being the warm companions of the single life into agents of divine (or demonic) retribution for our dreams of self-sufficiency. It's enough to make one think the storytellers fear women as much as they fear cats.

Because such stories are built on fear—fear of the unknown. It is our very strength, our completeness, that provokes this terror masquerading as scorn. It's a panic reaction that urges our enemies to dismiss our emotions as sentimentality, to scoff at our pairings, and to belittle us through jokes. They do so because they sense that the butt of their humor—we and our pets—are somehow larger than the domestic situations that frame us. That together we create a powerful whole. Like the long-ago pairing of the witch and her magical companion, the animal familiar, we and our pets are an enigma to these people. These jokers can sense that women and cats connect in ways few other creatures, animal or human, can, and that our union does not require anything from them. Such freedom leaves them with no means of controlling us, and for those who subsist on domination, such independence is uniquely threatening. Although they may camouflage their counterattacks with humor, under the laughs their intent is often vicious. Their laughter masks the resentment and jealousy stirred up by our bond. It masks their confusion. They cannot figure out what unseen understanding connects us, and that scares them.

Maybe they should be scared. And maybe, instead of being upset by such stories, we can learn to draw a little courage, a little pride, in knowing that we are powerful enough to provoke that vehement a reaction. This is our version of the love that dares not speak its name, and like the first brave souls who refused to closet other sorts of relationships, we, too, must reject the stigma and rejoice where we have been taught to feel shame. We mystify onlookers, especially those who expect women to be dependent on them, to be available and accessible at all times. And we can put that to use. Because fear, as any good hunting animal knows, has a scent, and by following it, by tracking down the jokes, we can find the source that feels so threatening to our critics. In this way, an urban myth like the one of the old woman and her cats can be seen as a shadow that by its darkness shows how bright and strong is the real connection. Clearly, if the relationship were not so powerful, so universal, it would not provoke such panic.

The kernel of our power, though, is not what they suspect. The core we are being warned away from is not a destructive or antisocial or even antimale force: it is simply the strength and depth of our personalities and of our capacity to love. Play the myth out, and you'll find the truth in the surprise ending. First, place it in a larger (and arguably more realistic) setting, and you'll see it reveals a much more complex and multifaceted relationship, not only between the teller and the audience, but between the principle characters, the solo woman and her cat. Take, for example, the recasting of the story on HBO's comedy *Sex and the City*. On that show, Miranda, one of the series' near-archetypal single, urban women, lives only with her pet. Like the unhappy woman of the original myth, Miranda is out to declare her independence, her need for nobody—no man—to complete her life. She has, in fact, just purchased her own home, a Manhattan co-op. But she is brought up short when someone repeats the urban myth to her, telling her about an elderly woman who also lived alone except for her cat, and who was missed by nobody and found long dead. The loneliness of her death, the conclusion of a solitary life, is stressed by the detail—passed on with glee—that by the time the woman's body was found, her face had been half-eaten by her beloved pet. In the next scene we see Miranda, still alone but for her cat, frantically pouring kitty crunchies into her pet's already overflowing bowl. Her cat, the sole rational creature in the scene, is happily feasting on the unexpected bounty and not, we should note, on the pretty, but nerve-ridden Miranda. The previously self-assured woman is now flustered by the idea of her independent life; the cat, as expected, is serene. And we all get a good chuckle, even us cat owners, as we see how yet again a woman is overindulging her pet puss to silence her own anxiety.

In this set-up, the kitty has shown itself to have what Colette called "the skull of a cruel beast," a toughness that compensates for its owner's insecurity. An animal behaviorist might add that its behavior is simply consistent with its species, *Felis domesticus*, and should not receive any more attention. But to dismiss the cat as simply the brave half, the unconcerned other, or as merely an animal is to miss the point entirely. For the small creature is Miranda's pet. It is living with Miranda by Miranda's choice. And that toughness, that animal fierceness, is precisely the point: Miranda's pet is now more than simply a cat. It is part of a functioning domesticity, part of a unit, and its demeanor must also now be considered in the context of the larger entity. Because we must remember that this cat-woman coupling is no accident: Miranda is a lawyer, a high-earning Manhattan professional who has *elected* to cohabit with a cool, collected cat. Although she now owns her own place, she did *not* adopt a high-strung toy dog or a high-maintenance exotic bird, and no matter how we project onto our pets, at some level we also accept and understand their essential animal nature. So we may assume that the cat's calm center, her implacable response to an uneasy world, is really indicative of Miranda's resilience, too—even if it feels better to have the kitty be the one to express it. The cat has simply acted out what Miranda, for many reasons, feels uneasy about revealing through her own body: she shows her poise, her calm, the self-assurance of an animal that can take care of itself. Looked at in this light, the humor fades, but finally we understand the warmth we felt even as we laughed. We recognize the deeper truth, and in our inner selves applaud the dynamic way that character and cat work together to function as one greater entity: an urban family of choice that can face the stone lonely city with a more complete acceptance of whatever comes along.

Complicated, yes, but no interaction with a cat is ever truly simple. And even those who refuse to see how two creatures can form complementary sides of one unit can find a lesson in this urban myth–turned–fairy tale: Whether they are stranded together by fate or bound by choice, these two city dwellers are finding a way to work out their issues together. And if they do so in a way that seems amusing to us, well, the fact that they can squeeze a few laughs out of a scary situation shows all of us yet again how deep this connection goes.

Of course, the humor in this scenario is of a common type, a superficial viewing that barely hints at the relationship's real depths. It mines what seems to the casual observer—to the non-cat-owners of the world—the apparently slapstick-rich gap between the much vaunted independence of our cats and the traditional, if loudly lamented, female role of submissiveness. Watching us, and ticking off the more than $22 billion we spend annually on our animal friends, they draw the conclusion that we are, by pandering to our animals, once again adopting the subservient role. We are, we often say, "owned" by our cats. We have all heard, we have all used, in that all-too-familiar apologetic tone, the term *codependent*, to describe our relations with our cats. That we, who have let ourselves be bossed around by our parents, by our employers, and too often by the lovers and partners who are in (or absent from) our lives, have ironically chosen pets who do the same.

Few of us will deny that our pets can be picky. However, just as Miranda's cat perhaps expressed her real inner calm, our kitty's "finicky" behavior may be expressing our own true emotions as well. Who, after all, would not sometimes want to be as discriminating as a cat? The original divas, cats let their companions know what they want—and what they will not tolerate—and, as a result, often get their way. Although we have been raised to be accommodating and flexible—to be "nice"—we, too, often feel haughty and disdainful. We, too, often want to express, to borrow a lioness's word, our pride. Why not act on these instincts, if not by active aggression then at least by the absence of fake positive, that is, affectionate, gesturings? Cats do not apologize, and many of us could take a lesson here. Although perhaps our old-fashioned sisters would disapprove, we know such behavior is healthier for us and usually a fairer way of dealing with others—as long as we are polite. (And cats, if we are capable of learning anything, are always more than happy to teach us how to walk away with grace and refinement.) In this mode, our pet's instinctive behavior may serve to reinforce an honest and useful, if sometimes less than socially acceptable, method of dealing with people.

In our cats, we find proof that discriminating behavior does not make one any less desirable. As any cat woman can attest, from our pets, from the years of play and scratches we have learned the feline use of distance as an enticement. We have witnessed, sometimes unwillingly, that silence can be more alluring than conversation. We pick up, from their examples, the seem-

ing paradox that a certain amount of space, as well as the willingness to stroke and be stroked, makes closeness possible over the
long run. Cats, perhaps more than any other house pet, are
known for their individuality and independence. Living in close
quarters with an animal who can remain totally self-possessed
while still being able to beg for table scraps is bound to impress
upon us the importance of dignity and of discretion, the additional weight a bit of distance gives to closeness when it comes,
not to mention the necessary role of privacy in a relationship of
trust and intimacy. "Cats love one so much," sums up author
Mary Wilkins Freeman. "But they have so much wisdom they
keep it to themselves."

From our cats, as well, we learn that honest warmth is a
virtue. While their critics may call these dear animals distant, we
know otherwise, having been the beneficiaries of their soft comfort. From such independent creatures, this quiet company—
those gentle, kneading purrs—is a great gift. No matter how
frightened we are of our own vulnerability, they seem to tell us
that sometimes we must let down our guards and curl up on a
friendly lap. This, too, is part of love. Emotional integrity is key
and helps us know when the time is right, for our pets instinctively understand that it does our souls no more good to fake an
aloof attitude than it does to pretend to an affectionate one.
From our cats we can learn the value of such emotional bravery,
of being an attentive and affectionate companion when the situation requires.

We have all heard tales of the solace and sympathy our kitties
can provide, and these emphasize how pain and loneliness can be
alleviated by a comforting presence. "When I was getting treatment for depression, she would allow me to hold her, and pet her
for longer durations than usual, and also be more physical with

her when I was very low," says Trisha, whose two cats have helped her through rough times. "To this day she literally licks my tears away."

Whether the sharing is always this dramatic, or simply the unexpected joy of a usually independent cat climbing into one's lap at the end of a trying day, we all know the pleasure such affection gives.

"I always had the stereotypic view of cats as aloof," recalls Robin, an active, athletic dog lover who has also grown to adore her cats Vinny and the late, great Buddy. "I knew of people who had very strong connections to their cats and I never understood it." Not until she moved into a roommate situation that came with a cat did she learn the difference. "I have this great memory of moving and this cat greeting us—she had this funny meow, she went *'meep, meep'*—and I discovered that cats could be affectionate and warm, and that won me over."

Such actions serve to affirm our own more generous tendencies, whether these be to make a check-in phone call or visit an ill friend. Yes, in the case of our cats, the behaviorists may argue about the consciousness of the decision to reach out. ("I think she may just like the salty taste," admits Trisha, reflecting on her cat's fondness for tears.) But no matter how generosity is rewarded, it clearly pays off for the one who shares the comfort, as well as the one who receives it. That's the payback for being a social animal. And while it is true that ongoing research is constantly uncovering more and more links between the big cats and our house pets, this research does not necessarily mean that our cats are bestial in the judgmental human sense. They are neither cold nor unnecessarily cruel. Many big cats, such as lions, are social beings, creatures who enjoy lounging and hunting together in family units. So who is to say that we have not become our cats' new prides, their families of choice? Perhaps they see us as their kittens to be encouraged or their peers to be cheered on. We know that they must be feeling some kind of bond with us as well; we sense the truth of this each time that flag of a tail brushes by our legs.

"I can't move now," I frequently tell my husband or friends on the phone. "Cyrus is kneading my arm." Sure this action, one heavy paw pushed into me after another, is probably a sign that he was weaned too early. (And it may be best for my marriage that I am unable to actually nurse my kitty.) I don't care. Those who know me and love me understand the joy I feel when Cyrus goes through this affectionate, if futile, action. They know how thrilled I am that this diminutive beast, this private house lion, is acting toward me as he did once to his own mother.

The point here, one which many outsiders miss, is not simply the range of contact between woman and pet. The point, the one we can most learn from, is the apparent mindfulness that guides these free and unencumbered choices. Sure, our cats are independent. Sure, they come and go and come again, not always when we call. That's the key to the relationship. Because the flip side is then true as well: No cat, no *real* cat (with an exception made here for a few particularly floppy Maine coons) can be held when he or she doesn't want to be, or be restrained in a lap when the floor is desired. Which means that when our cats are with us, when they are actively seeking out our presence or gracing our laps, it is because they have decided to do so. *Our cats choose to be with us.* And that choosing is both an honor and an excellent example of the kind of relationship we want and we deserve.

"There's only one thing I ever truly envied Thisbe for," my friend Anne says, talking about her thirteen-year-old tabby. "If there's one way I could be like her, it would be this: She really doesn't care what other people think of her." Of course she doesn't care what humans think, some might scoff. She's a cat.

But, well, that's the point. We cat folk don't want doggish fealty. We don't want to be forced to give it, and we don't want to receive it. We know we can buy affection, at least temporarily. What we want is to be chosen. And we want to be chosen by intelligent, well-kept-up, attractive individuals. We want to be chosen for who we are, complete with all our insecurities and waverings and all those lovely vulnerabilities that we have been taught to disdain in ourselves, and we are—by our cats.

Don't laugh, at least not yet. Instead, think about intimacy for a moment. Think about what we as warm-blooded creatures need from life. The desire for closeness, for connection, wrote pioneering psychiatrist John Bowlby, the progenitor of attachment theory, is essential for our survival as a species. The awareness of our need for others, our desire for their love and approval, he explains, is a sign that we have taken a step from the unconscious dependency of childhood toward a more conscious adulthood. Feminist and relational psychotherapists such as Judith V. Jordan have taken this theory further, postulating that through connection, through empathy, we heal and grow throughout our lives. In other words, it is adult to seek closeness. But by observing the choices of our cats, their innate sense of dignity and their unselfconscious possession of their own bodies, we learn that we too can (and do) make choices in relationships. Such a bonding as we want—a trust and closeness that also maintains our dignity and our integrity—is not possible without this acute sense of self. To be close to others, we must be comfortable in our own skins. As Harriet Lerner, Ph.D., writes in her relationship-dissecting *The Dance of Intimacy*, "intimacy means we can be who we are in a relationship."

True, cat owners are often accused of being insular rather than intimate, of preferring—like the old lady of the urban legend—our pets to people. And to be completely honest, sometimes we do; they are self-grooming after all, which is a distinct benefit over some people. But it is also true that a relationship with a cat is qualitatively different from a relationship with a person, and not necessarily inferior. Yes, those scornful and self-contained types who do not live with cats will scoff, some of us may be filling in blanks in our lives by lavishing "inappropriate" affection on out pets. We may be substituting cats for missing people, or supplying ourselves with what psychologists would call "transitional objects," making up for the absence of love or family with a four-footed replacement.

But such a simplification overlooks the special qualities a woman can find in the relationship with her pet. It dismisses the real intimacy between us, and thus the myriad possibilities for growth and connection—even with humans—that can and often do come of our bond with our pets. Because intimacy is at the core of our relationship with our cats. Who, after all, knows us so well as the creature who will drink out of our toilet? And because our connection is based on identity, rather than activity, it comes with a closeness that can only grow as we learn more about ourselves.

With our awareness of who we are comes our recognition of the quality of love to which we are entitled. Being loved by a pet can serve, as the psychological theorist Harry Stack Sullivan described it, as a "corrective relationship," a healing bond that helps us to work through unresolved conflicts, and ultimately sets the stage for healthier, more mutual human connections. It is true, although not in the way our critics would have it, that we practice many human roles in private with our pets. They are our best girlfriends, to whom we can complain when our time is torn between jobs or between managing the home and marriage. They may be our peers, and sometimes even our parents, who let us bounce ideas around and help us reach our own decisions.

"She's taught me to let go sometimes," says Dove of her cat Pounce DeLion. "I've learned patience. I've learned that sometimes things don't matter. That sometimes it is far more important to watch that bird fly."

Our cats are, in many healthy ways, extensions of our imagination and of ourselves. They walk before us. "She has allowed me to contemplate and deal with aging and loss issues," says Juli, who has seen her beloved pink-nosed Sophie grow old. And yes, our cats are often our children, when we do not have them or after they have left home. "Throughout her life, my cat has taught me incredibly simple and important lessons about responsibility, nurturing, and motherhood," continues Juli. "She has been my teacher."

Think about one of the cat's other mythic roles: that of the familiar, the magical companion who helps the witch woman access her powers. Or—to be less gothic about it—her un- or subconscious. It is true, a pet, any pet, can be a partner. However, by its particularly contemplative nature, a cat encourages us in thought and reflection. We watch a kitten playing, and we think about how we bide our time. We sit by a sleeping cat, and we settle into our own quiet. We look into those mysterious eyes, and we see ourselves. Such self-reflection, far from being isolating, lays the groundwork for any kind of healthy bonding, for growth and creativity. For whether we live by ourselves or with roommates, with a partner, mate, or children, we still need time to be alone and yet not-alone. Like the witches of Salem who were probably, just like us, thoughtful women who took pleasure in contemplating kitty on the hearth, we need time for our own dreams. Perhaps even more in this busy century, we need time for thought, and ways to amuse ourselves by ourselves; we need space in which to replenish our imaginations with daydreams and with no dreams at all. And no matter whether we have confidantes close by or family within our walls, we all still seek out a reflection of our feelings, a calm pool into which we can pour our thoughts at day's end, or in the morning stillness before others have risen. Our cats give us this and other gifts. In the quiet space between the waves of a purr we work out our issues, find warmth when we are lonely, safety when we are scared, pride when we feel timid and beaten down, and grace when we find our workday lives—or ourselves—too ugly.

"Women, poets, and especially artists, like cats," wrote the painter Helen Winslow. "Delicate natures only can realize their sensitive nervous systems." We find, in our closeness to our cats, our own centers. With cats, we learn to appreciate our own mysteries. You could say, if you will run the risk of being burned, that we modern-day cat women use cats as did our elder sisters in Salem, as our mediums—what veterinary ethologist Myrna Milani calls our "psychological familiars." Our feline companions serve as the cool, collected channelers who help us locate and concentrate our own creative magic, who help us midwife our dreams by simply observing, with an air of approving calm. The cat lover Colette put it rather well when she wrote "the only risk you ever run in befriending a cat is enriching yourself." With our cats we become better at, as intimacy expert Harriet Lerner puts it, "being who we are."

This aspect of our relationship can be difficult, not in the least because of what it teaches us about our own weaknesses. And, painfully, about our own mistakes. I will never forget, even if Cyrus has, our first New Year's Eve. We should have been together. Hell, I don't remember having another date. But I had miscalculated. Two days before the holiday, I had taken my six-month-old companion into the local cat hospital to be neutered

(I still find it difficult to say "castrated"). And somehow either I had misunderstood the length of his stay, or perhaps simply the days the hospital would be open for the routine business of discharging a small, feline patient. For whatever reason, I found myself hanging on the phone while a technician repeated her news: Yes, Cyrus would have to remain in the hospital over New Year's Eve. The surgery would be routine, and I wasn't to have any worries, but I would not be able to pick up my newly socially acceptable companion until January 2. As I recall, I fell silent at that, and the hospital technician must have heard something in that air space, a sigh of dejection or perhaps she simply sensed my remorse, because—in that perky fashion that people who work in hospitals have—she then tried to cheer me up. "Don't worry about your kitten while he's with us," she said to me, her voice taking on a lilt. "We're going to have a party for all the animals who have to stay in over the holiday. We'll have music and dancing . . ." She paused, perhaps for the first time reviewing my pet's chart. "And for those who've already had their operations, there'll be intellectual conversation groups. And chess."

Chess. I knew there was a friendly intent behind her joke, but I couldn't laugh just then. I thought of my playful puffball sitting in a cage over the holiday and my heart sank. But when I picked him up two days later and he purred and batted at my finger, I realized that he was not emotionally wounded by a weekend in a box. He was simply happy to be home. And that even if I had messed up the scheduling in the process, I had also done what was necessary. It was time—he was already teaching me—to forgive myself and move on. And so we did.

All through that first year, Cyrus ate and grew and in the process raised some serious issues for me. The fuzzy creature I had adored for his batlike perfection had, it turned out, both worms and fleas as well as an annoying tendency to spew waste from both ends, and the money I expended on subsequent vet bills outweighed anything I had yet spent, or could afford to spend, on myself. And so I learned to spend more freely, which was arguably a good thing because it forced me to confront questions of worth and property—not to mention budgeting and the priorities that emerge when one shares one's life with another. Specifically priorities that required that I learn to quell my disgust and clean up whatever mess my pint-size friend could provide, ideally before the roommates came home or my parents came to visit.

Ultimately, these lessons paid off in all my relationships. Over the ensuing years, as my life changed, as I dated and traded in men and jobs and lifestyles, Cyrus served as a feline barometer against which I could measure myself—and the people I chose to be my, our, intimates. For when I met the man who I thought could prove to be the one I'd hoped for, I found my favorable initial opinion elevated by my cat's acceptance of this new alpha male. And, to be completely honest, by his liking for my cat. The traits I valued in Cyrus—his seeming willfulness, the thought that appears to precede each movement from window to couch, the contrast between his self-sufficiency and the obvious vulnerability of size—drew this man, too, and by that point, perhaps, I had learned enough about myself to know that this mattered to me. Need it be said that my human mate shared many of the characteristics of my cat beyond even the physical similarities that my long-ago roommate had predicted? That he was sweet, contemplative, and willing to attempt communication despite our many differences? No, unlike a growing number of pet owners, we didn't give Cyrus a role in our wedding. (He hates crowds.) But we did think about it.

However, before I agreed to share my life with this man, I had to face up to the consequences of sharing my beloved pet. As any woman who has bonded with her cat will recognize, this may have been one of the more difficult trials for me. For this man also enjoyed stroking that diamond-shaped little head. He, too, understood the honor Cyrus did him the first time the cat sat by him, not to mention the first time Cyrus kneaded his belly when he lay on the couch. And that was when I had to ponder not only whether *my* cat had become *our* cat, but what pet ownership—our own type of monogamous fidelity—meant to me.

The transition was loaded. The first time I watched the two cuddle, my pet settling onto my boyfriend's belly and closing his eyes for a nap, I felt myself flooded by a hot-lava outpouring of jealousy and pettiness. Insecurities I thought long since quelled raised their heads, causing me to fret about not measuring up. About being replaced in the affections of my longtime pet by my newfound mate. Through my affection for my kitty, I had discovered my very own form of commitment anxiety: I was tempted to grab the cat and run. But when the emotional storms finally subsided, I found I was really just facing the same basic questions that surface in all relationships. I realized that I had to look at Jon and at Cyrus and—deeply, honestly—at myself, and consider how much of what mattered to me, really, did I want to share? How much was I willing to open up? Because for me, as perhaps for every woman who cares deeply about her pet, sharing a cat serves as an excellent metaphor for sharing a life. My life, as well as Cyrus's. And I saw, once again, how much of myself was invested in this relationship with my cat and how much, over the years, I had learned from him about my own dynamics. For our cats, I have come to believe, can teach us more about ourselves when they are curled up sleeping on a pillow than many of us will ever garner from years on a psychiatrist's couch.

Ultimately this knowledge—the gift of this bond—not only helps us settle into our place in the world, it helps us accept the processes through which we will all go in our own lives. We cannot be other than who we honestly are when we are with our cats. We instinctively do not want to be. And, therefore, if we spend any time with cats at all, we must then also come to accept our own inept humanity. We must learn to face the cool appraisal in those intense gold (or green or gray) eyes, and forgive ourselves for only doing our best.

"What is he thinking?" my husband routinely asks me, when Cyrus gets up for no apparent reason and, after staring at the wall for a few minutes, saunters out of the room. "He's going to work on his memoirs," I usually reply. And although I invariably remain on the sofa, the TV turned on and the newspaper spread out across my lap, wasting at least another hour that will leave me tired in the morning, I know why I have answered in this fashion. Cyrus is, to my mind, doing what I should be doing, without guilt and without coercion. And when I retreat sometime later to find him curled into a gray disc, asleep on the bed, I recognize that once again he has acted as I should have done, and I admire his wisdom.

2

BONDING

"My cats all came to me with the exception of my 'first born,' Foo Foo," explains the petite Sharon, who even at her full height of five feet can be almost overwhelmed by her nine felines. "Foo Foo I chose: My neighbor rescued a pregnant cat and she had seven kittens. I went to look at them and they were all adorable. I went to her apartment daily to play with the kittens and figure out which one suited my personality best. As I studied each kitten's behavior, I noticed that one in particular was very prissy. She didn't walk—she pranced. She was kind of a snob and was very picky about who petted her. I thought, 'Perfect, she's just like me! I'll take her.' "

If we followed the advice of the experts, our methods of choosing cats would be a logical, almost scientific process that selected the best socialized, more adaptable kittens of any litter to become our lifelong pals. We would spend time observing the litter coolly, looking for the most active or the intelligent kitten. We would follow the excellent advice of books like Cats for Dummies, which recommends bringing along a cat toy to the shelter, or wherever the choice will be made, for "personality testing" the kittens. "Never get a kitten on impulse," authors Gina Spadafori and Paul D. Pion advise, which means, roughly, test driving them for levels of awareness, energy, and socialization in order to select the kitten that will grow up to bring the right amount of activity and attention to our homes. All kittens are adorable, they warn, but to find a compatible pet for life we should be ruthless about rejecting even the cutest ones if, when offered a feather toy or an open lap, they don't seem quite up to par.

While we all may begin with such unimpeachable intentions, as far as I can tell this kind of kitty critique very rarely happens. Instead, we find ourselves identifying with the little creatures, often because of their shyness or their neediness as much as their abundant energy or their beauty. We see traits that remind us of ourselves, or of how we wish to be. We project like mad, and we fall in love.

What is the magic that makes this happen? Often enough, as happened with me and Cyrus, the connection is immediate. Sometimes, as with Lynne, it isn't even wanted.

"It was, however, a sweet moment," she writes me. "And inevitable. I was at a co-worker's house in November for a small after-work gathering when she told a bunch of us we had to see the new kittens. Her cat had gotten out of the house and had a second litter shortly after they placed all the cats from the first litter. She made a point of trying to get me to take one because she knew I liked cats and was now living alone. I kept saying I would love to but that I couldn't have one in my apartment." Lynne, a tall, cool blonde with several graduate degrees should have been smart enough to sense trouble. She stayed anyway.

"And then my co-worker placed this tiny black-and-white furball with a pink nose on my lap, and it slept on me and crawled on me all night. Well, I knew then what was going to happen, and told her I'd take this kitty when it was weaned. I wasn't supposed to have a cat, but I kept thinking, 'I can hide her from the land-lord.'" That was all it took, and the two have cohabited hap-pily—in a new apartment—since.

Our cats have their own say on the subject. As I type this, Cyrus is walking across my computer. While I was opening up this file, he jumped to the sofa beside me and then stepped neatly by my hands and onto my laptop. Carefully placing one velvet paw before the other, he has walked above the keys and across the space bar to take up a seat beside me, and then pawed delicately at the book lying by my side. Seeing what he was up to, I removed the book to the table and pushed the laptop a bit far-ther away from my body. He muttered what I interpret as satis-faction at my making room for him, a soft *"mr-r-ah"*—half aspiration, half mew—as he turned and kneaded the part of my hip left exposed by the laptop, before settling down beside me to purr and, probably, to sleep as I work.

Cyrus has developed a new set of personality traits as he has aged, and I find myself adjusting to him, to his emerging elder-statesman personality, much as I did to the rambunctious kitten that I adopted out of my friend Kathei's litter more than sixteen years before. These days we toss around the catnip toys a lot less. A few nights ago I did let the belt of my terry-cloth robe dangle, afraid to hope, and was thrilled when he stalked and pounced on it as in the old days, that dragging bit of cloth becoming once more the most elusive of prey. But such moments of play are fewer now, and more often I find myself sitting beside my old friend, sometimes stroking him as he stares into space and sometimes watching him sleep. He seems to desire my presence more these days, even if it's just to remain at the breakfast table a few minutes longer while he surveys the yard from the kitchen window, to share attack strategies for the squirrels that brazenly stare back from the lawn, and to size up birds made more visible by the falling leaves. I tarry longer now, waiting for him to tire of his watch and find a comfortable place to curl up and nap, or for him to remove himself from my presence of his own will for reasons that I cannot begin to guess. I want to just be with him more now, as he too experiences autumn.

We make a quiet couple these days, and that is a comfort to me. Some of this, I know is fear of loss, fear of the inevitable that I can't avoid each time I pick up his diminished bulk, or feel the bones of his spine and pelvis as I stroke his gently vibrating back. Some, though, comes from him, from his seemingly increased desire to be with me, to find me in the room nearby when he wakes up. Often I am; I want him to be happy, and he usually seems to know that I will be there, or will be only a room or a hallway away. He wasn't always so confident, and these days when he wakes and seeks me out, at work or sitting with a book, I remember such a time. Once, when a kitten, during a visit to my parent's house he woke up in my old bedroom alone and believed himself lost, abandoned as he slept. I had gone downstairs and left him sleeping there, a perfect silver circle of fur arranged neatly on the coverlet. I'm ashamed to say I thought little about him as I chatted on the phone downstairs, calling old acquaintances and making plans—until I heard the plaintive cry, the *"ow!"* of a lost, lonely kitten. *"OW!"* was ringing ridiculously loudly from up the stairs. *"OW!"*

"Cyrus, what's wrong?" I remember responding, putting down the receiver to run to the foot of the stairs. "Cyrus!" And standing at the top of the tall staircase, eyes blinking still from sleep, was my kitten. He was calm again, looking down at me, having been drawn most likely by the sound of my voice and been comforted by the sight of me, by the assurance of my presence. *"Mr-up-up-up,"* he chattered as he made his way down the steep stairs, each step taller than his round baby body was long. His voice had become chatty, almost conversational. And as much as I can know anything about a cat, I am convinced he had wakened alone in a strange place and panicked. My voice and then the sight of me calmed him immediately, and he hopped his way downstairs to continue exploring this new territory, confident in the security of my continued presence.

Cyrus was always a people cat. Early on, I attributed his desire for my company to his first experiences with my kind and his own. My kitten, who grew up so handsome, was the runt of his litter, less energetic than his peppy siblings, smaller and less healthy, and I chose him for all the wrong reasons. When Kathei's momma cat had her litter and my friend invited me over, I probably should have opted for one of the livelier babies, one of the other gray or black or orange furballs that ran toward me or fled, chasing a noisy toy, or that ignored me entirely to nurse lustily. But my heart was taken by the one who remained when Kathei and I and her daughter loomed over the cluster of kittens. For as some scattered onto the rug and one or two others dug into their momma's belly seeking a nipple, one tiny gray kitten just sat and looked up at me. I felt chosen.

Afterward, I told myself that this kitten might end up ignored by its mother or bullied by its bigger, stronger peers and that was reason enough for my solicitous care. Sure enough, when I brought my new pet home a few weeks later, my roommate's irascible adult cat, Chenille, responded thus. Not that Chenille, a rather neurotic and overweight calico whose name I have changed to protect those who undoubtedly loved her, beat up on Cyrus. Rather she seemed resentful, even paranoid, and if I seem to be somewhat the same in my description of her I rest easy believing that other new mothers would judge a similar bully the same way. For what Chenille did was cruel, but also rather odd, and convinced me that she was not an emotionally healthy cat.

Chenille, with all of a big three-bedroom apartment to choose from, seemed to decide that she couldn't share her litter box with Cyrus. Not her food, perhaps because I soon realized that I needed to provide private dishes. Not her bed; Cyrus shared mine. But her litter box. Now I have since learned that such territoriality might not be unusual, but I still believe that older cat's mode of enforcement was. To protect her turf, quite literally, Chenille would sit in the litter box for hours. She would just squat there, waiting, and hiss at my little fellow whenever he tried to approach. This is my box, the last bastion of my privacy, that fat, ornery cat hissed. Go away.

I should have realized there was more going on here than just feline politics. At twenty-three, I also should, perhaps, have been wiser in the ways of people, and of roommates. Because by the time I had gotten my kitten—without, I will admit, getting more than grudging conditional acceptance from my then-roommates—I had already begun to have my own problems with our shared living quarters.

First there was the problem of the sewing room, as the large apartment's dining room had come to be known. With a big table in the kitchen, and—to be honest—with many of our meals eaten in front of the TV in the living room, this sunny room lit by its big windows and door onto our porch had come to be used as a workroom. When I moved in, the newcomer joining a long-settled unit of two, I had observed the central table strewn with papers and cloth, seen the sideboard piled high with books and catalogues, and figured that it was a common workspace, a catch-all back-of-the-building room outside our bedrooms and separate from the tidy living room, which guests could see as soon as they came through our front door.

Since I wrote rather than sewed in my spare time, I figured I could stake out a corner of the room for my own work, specifically for my computer and printer. That was my hobby, I figured, though in my heart I was always hoping that the words I churned out would take me away from the chemical smells and triplicate reports of pithed cats. (I briefly worked as a secretary in a physiology lab. Don't ask.) Therefore, one afternoon when I'd gotten home, I set about moving my equipment from my tiny crowded bedroom into that sunny space. First I carried in the dowdy blue Kaypro that I wrote my essays and reviews on, a heavy boxlike computer that would have dwarfed today's machines (except for its minuscule, recessed screen) but which, even with its gray metal stand, took up less space than their Singers and notion boxes, not to mention the dressmaker's dummies that stood nearby. Then I carried in my carton of printer paper, which sat neatly below the printer, and threaded the first page through the old-style dot matrix printer's jaws, ready to go. When I stepped back into the doorway, my entire setup nearly disappeared in the colorful mess made by bolts of cloth, by pattern books and patterns. Good, I thought, I'm fitting in. I was ready to work. This was not to be.

"What is all this *machinery* doing here?" I remember hearing from my room as I changed from my secretarial skirt and hose. "What are all these papers?"

"That's my computer," I tried to explain. "I thought I'd move my work stuff into the work room."

"But it's the *sewing* room!"

"Yeah, but I don't sew."

"It's for sewing!" We might have gone back and forth longer, but I doubt it. At twenty-three, I lacked the confidence to argue further. My move into the supposed common space had been rejected, and the computer and its paraphernalia moved back into the one room to which my share of the rent inarguably gave me rights.

Then there was the question of curfew. Not that we had one, not that we'd ever discussed one. But at that age, I had the energy, the desire, and the camaraderie to go out fairly often, and certainly on the weekends. To top it off, I was finally getting assignments from the local paper to write about some of the bands I saw and heard, musicians whom I met and drank with until closing time. My roommates at the time were less social. One had a steady boyfriend, but they usually stayed in. And the other, well, she would sometimes hit the bars after work and would sometimes try blind dates. But every time the phone rang and it wasn't for her, her resentment was made obvious by her terse, often inaccurate messages. And every time I went out buffed and polished and woke up glowing from whatever adventures or substances the night had brought my way, my good mood added fuel to her simmering jealousy.

The problem became focused, I soon found, on my (to me very reasonable) behavior of sleeping late on Saturday mornings, catching up on my rest after a full week of work and, usually, nights of play. Even though we were all in our twenties, all healthy, and more or less single, such a life, clearly, was not acceptable to my unattached flatmate, who not only began to get up earlier and earlier to start her Saturday cleaning, but began ramming the vacuum cleaner against my door as soon as the cleaning commenced. Hard. I got the message, and although I didn't stop staying out late with my friends, I did begin wearing earplugs to bed.

No wonder then, that their shared cat acted as she did. Chenille, fat and irritable, was simply following her owners' cues when she hissed at my kitten or cuffed him as he bent toward the food dishes in the kitchen corner. But when Chenille began spending increasing amounts of time performing her most perverse habit, that of hoarding the litter box, my Cyrus, the runt of his litter and certainly the smallest and newest inhabitant of our apartment, took action.

"CLEA!" I heard the bellow even through the earplugs early the next morning. "GET IN HERE RIGHT NOW!" My roommate's voice was coming from the bathroom and so I stumbled from my slumbers into the small room at the end of the hall. I have never seen a woman more red in the face. She stared at me. I tried to focus. She gestured downward, into the sink, her hand still holding the toothbrush she had obviously just picked up. There, in the basin, was a neat pile of turds. Cyrus was nowhere to be found.

Now, in retrospect I wonder that we both accepted that my cat had made the mess. After all, even when one cat is still growing and the other mature, once first kittenhood is past their turds do not look that different. Clearly, my roommate had assumed the worst, as she would put it, because I was the unruly newcomer and therefore my pet must be the more bestial of the two. And I? Well, I had seen how the bigger, older cat had tried to bully my kitten, and if I didn't yet have the self-possession to champion myself, I instinctively bristled to defend my pet. Plus in my heart of hearts I admired the solution that I believed Cyrus's innate intelligence had found: He had, after all, defecated in a basin, in a contained space, as near to the litter box as he was allowed to get. The fact that he made a statement about our presence in the apartment was another thing altogether, and I am not entirely certain that it was not a conscious gesture on my tiny feline friend's part.

However, in this situation I too was the runt, or at least the one with the least power. And though I tried not to share the wisdom and humor I saw in his actions, as I cleaned up the shit, I was already laughing. Nothing would beat the look on that woman's face, I told myself, and that was worth all. Cyrus and I moved out a month or two later, but if there had been any doubt about our relationship before, our bond was cemented from that morning on.

I should pause here to discuss Chenille, since she too was a cat and she too was bonded with a woman, primarily the happier of my two roommates. She was, in my biased view, an extremely neurotic cat, overweight to the point of unhealthiness and unfriendly to anyone who was not her one person. But perhaps she had reason. Perhaps she came from a bad home, and perhaps my roommate was the one person who cared—the sympathetic soul who rescued her and gave her love and clearly fed her all she wanted. I look back on her and see an ordinary tabby, her subtle tiger stripes dimmed in my memory by her offensive behavior. But the beauty, and the bond, was not, in this case, for me.

After all, when Cyrus first came into my life he wasn't yet the furry sweetheart he would become. He was a small kitten with a big spirit, and staked a lion-size claim on my heart, but he was more than a bit awkward. Even when we moved into our next place, with the much more amiable Susan, he had his share of mishaps: I can still hear his howling as the cloth front of my stereo speaker became dislodged during his ascent up the tall cabinet's front. Despite my quick run down the hall, I didn't get there in time to catch it, or dislodge his panicked claws, and he was still clinging as the cloth-covered frame fell over, bearing his small frame with it. And I remember the time either Susan or I had forgotten to replace the fireplace screen and Cyrus decided to explore that previously forbidden space. We returned home to find perfect, rounded soot prints all over the rug, around the bathtub, and along the kitchen counters where he would never dare venture in my presence.

Until he filled out under my care, he went through a period of looking a tad ratty, too, his mite-bitten ears scratched into scabs and his green eyes runny and sad. The cat he grew into couldn't have been less a misfit, or more handsome. "What is his breeding?" I've often been asked. "Is he a show cat?" After perusing countless cat books and matching his smoky, slightly tiger-striped back, wide gray-and-white ruff, and elegantly plumed tail to one such specialty breed, I'm often tempted to respond that, yes, he is a show cat. A Norwegian Forest Cat, bred for his fine coat and green eyes, the intelligent point of his face and large tufted ears. But the truth is, of course, that he's a mix, just like 90 percent of the pet cats in this country.

And while others admire a magnificent beast with a proud ruff, with a flag of a tail that arches up in an elegant sweep of long, silky hair, they do not always see the cat I do. They never notice, for example, how his leonine profile veers from the classic into a slightly bumpy nose. They don't see that my perfect showcat has a Roman nose, rather like mine. A Brando nose that, had I not known better, would have hinted to me of a misspent youth and boxing rings. And as much as I admire Cyrus's lush coat, his stunning tail and ears, over the years it is that nose I have come to love most of all, savoring the times he would let me stroke its dark smoked velvet. Yes, he's a handsome cat, marvelously so, but I would love him no less were he still bat-faced and scrawny. He's my cat, and that's what makes him special.

⁂

Most of us have a similar tale of bonding, sometimes beyond expectations.

"I'm not allergic to all cats," says Karen. "But you just can't tell till you get them home." For that reason, Karen had been hesitant about getting a kitten of her own, despite a lifelong love of felines. Fate stepped in in the form of a golden-brown tabby she met outside a neighborhood convenience store. "This cute little cat was going up to everybody," Karen recalls, describing the plump tabby as she greeted shoppers, curling around one ankle and then another. "She had the cutest little face, but she had no collar." The store staff didn't know her, and so when Karen next returned and the young cat was still there, the warm-hearted redhead took her in—temporarily. "I took photos and made posters asking, 'Is this your cat?' I took her to the vet. Nobody claimed her."

Just as well. "I wasn't sure if I'd be allergic to her, but I found it didn't bother me, and she was the most affectionate little cat in the world." Since the day that cat, Shayna, came into her life, Karen has also adopted the green-eyed Samantha Mulder and learned to love her boyfriend Eric's cat, the smoke tabby Handsome, as well.

That connection with Shayna, however, was special. "I'd had a family cat growing up," Karen recalls her New York girlhood. "But I realized that although Bingo loved me, she was really my mother's cat. So this was my first cat. Shayna was *my* cat."

For Mary, the impetus to connect came out of primal rage, as her better nature sprang forth to protect a helpless kitten.

"I first saw her in June; she'd been born in May," recalls Mary, rescuer of Boo, the scared and underweight kitten she first espied in a friend's building. "She was one of a litter that had been dropped off with this group of people who lived in the basement." Her voice grows cold as she describes the enclave of squatters, rowdy drunks who scared the young professional. They were always hanging around the building's stoop, she recalls, brawling with each other or trying to cadge money from passersby. With all their drinking and fighting, they were beyond caring for themselves, let alone any animals. "I used to run by their door when it was open. I was so afraid of seeing them," she remembers, her voice dropping to a whisper.

But even though she found the people frightening, her occasional glimpses of the skittish white kitten began to rouse other feelings as well. And although Mary's lease clearly specified "no pets," she started to think about the small creature she'd see occasionally in that den of horror.

Not that the petite public-relations professional was looking for a cat. She was, in fact, more of a self-described dog person, an active, achievement-oriented type. "I had grown up with dogs," she explains. "I thought dogs were more valuable, because they were more productive, and in my family that was important." As a child, Mary had worked for animal welfare groups, pitching in at shelters to help lost or hurt animals. But when she donned the responsibilities of adult life, she put aside such efforts, telling herself they were wasted. Instead, she structured her days around results, around an energetic extroversion. Her early success in publicity reflected her efforts to look good, to sound smart, and to deliver the goods, no matter what the cost. Taking in an animal would use up some of the time usually allocated to working out or finding that perfect Armani suit. It did not make sense in her go-go scheme.

For more than a month, therefore, she watched the drama under the stairs. The horror grew: The drunks below the stairs grew bored with the kitten's normal antics—and so they put her in a clothes dryer, probably more than once. Mary heard them laughing. "They thought that was really funny cause her hair would stand up from the static electricity." Then one morning she saw that the skinny snow white kitten was marked with blood—and mutilated. It seems in their alcoholic haze the squatters had thought they could make some money off the kitten by cutting off her tail and selling her as a Manx.

Mary was shocked, but still held back by the combination of fear and preoccupation with her own life. Then, one morning, she happened by as another atrocity seemed about to happen. "I was down there one day and I saw this little fur ball sort of scuttering under the furniture to try to get away. And I heard this guy saying something about how cats are a waste, they are useless. And this poor thing . . ." She pauses.

"Something inside me snapped. I saw this animal and it was a paradigm shift. I realized that part of me had always loved animals and cared about them, and something changed." She forgot her fear. She stepped between the kitten and its tormentor, her five feet and change facing his six-plus. He moved to push her out of the way. "And I saw this happening—and I just slugged him."

"That's it," Mary remembers saying to herself. "I don't care what happens, I'm taking the cat. And that was the beginning of our life together." (Boo's tormentor threatened to sue the small but feisty woman. In retrospect, Mary wishes he had: such a suit would have given her a chance to expose his despicable treatment of the cat. However, his threat came to nothing; he was— like many bullies—too much of a coward to take on an active, capable woman.)

Boo, named by Mary's young niece, didn't immediately respond to Mary's kindness. "She was a mess," her owner admits. With reason. "She was so angry, she'd just hiss at people and swat at them. My sister called her Devil Kitty." Over the next few months, however, the young cat realized she was safe, that not all humans were awful, cruel creatures.

"Ordinarily, she slept in one of the guest rooms on the bed. Then one night, four or five months into the relationship she jumped up on my bed and slept on me. I didn't touch her. I didn't look at her. I thought, 'Okay, this is cool.'

"From then on we were inseparable. We'd talk—well, I'd talk and she'd listen. Wherever I was she'd be. I'd set up a place in the kitchen for her, and she'd sit and watch me cook and do dishes." In time, Boo came to be the doyenne of Mary's home, twelve wooded acres she bought out in the country where she could cohabit with all the animals she loved. Boo indulged the other cats that Mary subsequently rescued, and even tolerated dogs from her rightful position as queen of Mary's heart. Boo passed away last year, at the age of twenty-one, but the emotions she sparked in Mary remain.

"Something inside of me changed because of Boo," she says. "From there on I realized I couldn't be false. You can have an image of yourself—and I'm in the image business and that's great—but if the substance isn't there, it doesn't matter. I learned that if you went back to the things you loved as a child in your heart you'd be who you truly are. Boo brought me back to who I was."

For Mary, the bond started with sympathy and resulted in enlightenment, a return to the values of her childhood. For Janice, the love of a cat offered a chance to grow beyond an outdated phobia.

Five years ago, Janice was afraid of cats. Seeing her now, a big, tall woman crawling under a Dumpster to lay out food dishes for a colony of feral cats, it is difficult to believe that she couldn't stand their look, couldn't stand what she calls "that glow in their eye." Although Janice is now one of the dedicated volunteers who make up Town Cats, a Maryland rescue organization that cares for feral and abandoned cats, five years ago she wasn't so openhearted, or so brave. "I had no use for cats," as she puts it.

She has since learned that they have a use for her. "Our major crisis right now is trapping about three hundred cats at the race-track," she says, explaining the process of capturing the feral and abandoned cats in order to neuter them and get them the most basic of vaccinations. She also volunteers at a temporary sanctuary that Town Cats runs for ferals. "We clean that one day a week," she says. "That takes about six hours."

For Janice, the turnaround came when she saw a notice at a local garden center saying "free kitten with each purchase." She'd already picked out her seeds and tools, and decided she'd take a peek at the bargain baby being offered. "It looked harmless," she says. The clumsy kitten, scooped from a cardboard box behind the counter, lacked the stare that so terrified Janice in adult cats. "So I took it home, and I loved it." She pauses, still surprised by her reaction. "I loved it! And I thought, I should give it a brother, so I made another purchase and got another kitten. And then they grew into cats."

That could have been a problem. But by this point the kitten-smitten Janice discovered she no longer feared the adult felines. These fierce-eyed beasts had, after all, emerged from her own harmless kittens. "But I missed having kittens so I went to the humane society and got two more," she explains. Janice was hooked.

An advertisement in a newspaper asking for donations of cat food led her to Town Cats. "I brought in a big bag of Purina, and they said 'thank you' and they asked if I knew what Town Cats was about." Not long after that, the divorced homemaker was spending time with Town Cats, helping the ferals and strays that the group adopts.

Between her own cats and the rescue work, Janice discovered the wonders of adult cats, too. "There is not a mean adult cat," she admits now. "They're afraid. They have been through so much and they have had to fend for themselves for so long, they just don't trust human beings." She now lives with her own four adult cats, whom she loves, and three foster ferals that she is trying to socialize so they can become adoptable too. "I came to terms with the fact that the fear does not have to be in me, it's in them already."

For me, the connection is about communication, about believing that this creature is trying to talk to me, and about my efforts to understand him across all the barriers between us.

These days it's automatic: I'll be sitting at the kitchen table, the newspaper open before me, when I realize I'm not alone. The house is quiet, but at my feet, looking up at my face, is the small gray cat I'd left asleep on his chair—as much as all chairs are his—a little while ago. He sees me turn toward him; I don't know how long he's been waiting. "Eh," he seems to say, with the nearly silent aspiration of a mew that seems to carry so much more portent in its lack of volume. "Eh." He waits for my response. "I'm only eating cereal. Do you want some?" He doesn't reply and I leave my breakfast and my paper to stir the food in his dish that was fresh only an hour or so before. He follows me, and once my attentions are completed, crouches down to enjoy his own breakfast, now moist and aromatic again as it was when he woke me for the first serving. Then, he had to pound on a magazine I'd improvidently left bedside to get my attention. This time, since I'm fully awake, telepathy serves, aided by that semisilent mew. "Eh," he says to me, green eyes fixed on me to make sure I understand. And I do.

Does any pet owner find this strange? I'm sure some do. The ones who refer to our animals of choice as "only cats," who think that these petite panthers aren't real pets because they have free will, would scoff at that story. They're the ones who roll their eyes at any mention of interspecies communication, who tell me that my cat only loves me because I feed him. They're the ones who will dismiss me as one of those women, one of those cat women who, lacking a child or a real vocation, lavishes undue affection on a thankless beast. A few years ago, they would also have brought up my manlessness, dismissing the closeness between Cyrus and me as misdirected desires for affection and physical contact. They would be snide and openly conde-scending. They would feel, at best, embarrassed for me, going public about my great need for this small animal companion and my belief in the bond that exists between us. They would think I was fooling myself, overcompensating, or overly fanciful. They would be wrong.

The bond between a woman and a cat is not a replacement for bonds with fellow humans, although often it is one of the few consolations of lonely and neglected women. It is not a substi-tute for sex, or for mothering, and there are even times when the push of a cool, wet nose against our skin, a sleek head rubbed against a hand, cannot compensate for intelligent compan-ionship of the human kind.

It does, however, provide a kind of closeness that respects the natures of both parties—and allows for the kind of freedom and mutual understanding that can be lacking in our bipedal society. No cat, for example, will ever say that you look like you gained weight. No cat will complain when you spend the day in bed. (In fact, both of these conditions are likely to endear you all the more to your favorite feline. The extra avoirdupois, the additional hours spent reclining simply make us more comfortable and accessible for their kneading and cuddling pleasure.) What we receive is more than an absence of censure. Unlike dogs, which seem to await our cues, cats have that marvelous sense of self that allows us to indulge ourselves as ourselves, confident in the belief that we are in the presence of intelligent but accepting creatures.

In truth, just how much of this bonding is pure projection is unclear. For me, Cyrus has always been in part a little man, a miniature human in a fur coat, a term more than one of my interview subjects has also used. His manners, the slight hesitation before he leaps or settles down or even begins kneading my arm or my lap, lends itself to the idea that he is thoughtful. The way his part-Siamese face seems to come to a point, ears tilted slightly forward, as he sniffs the bottom of a pants cuff or the sole of a visitor's shoe lends credence to my old roommate Susan's supposition that he is, like her, a scholar, an academic, an intellectual. Of course, it's very easy to view a cat, almost any cat, as a deep thinker once they settle into adulthood and start to spend most of their lives staring out windows or meditating on the sofa. Before that, when they are still chasing (and occasionally catching) their tails, it's hard to view them as anything other than fur-suited clowns. But with maturity, most cats seem to take on a gravity that casts them as philosophers, legislators, or, perhaps, counselors.

"He's a professor, certainly," said Susan one day. She was in graduate school at the time, so I bowed to her greater expertise in such matters. "A professor of smells. The Harvard College

Professor of Smellology." Certainly the title fit. With his quiet
calm and his wide-set green eyes, Cyrus appeared to be thinking
deep thoughts constantly and when he stopped to sniff something or someone, pausing for a few moments before moving on,
he did seem to be musing, to be cataloging and sorting the infor-
mation received. "He's putting that one away for later," Susan
would say as he once more sniffed at her new boot and then
slowly walked away, the contemplative look still on his face.

Maybe he was. I'm not one to scoff at the interior life of animals, even those who must (in the words of some long-forgotten
nature show) sleep or rest 80 percent of the time. Sure our darling kitties have brains the size of walnuts, but who is to say that
those cranial nuts are not being philosophically deployed,
dreaming dreams that we could barely grasp? Who is to say that
at any given time Cyrus is not, as I often maintain, working on
his memoirs?

The fact that I have been similarly employed as well, and am
likewise prone to staring into space if not openly napping, may
perhaps play into this interpretation. But isn't such identification
one of the beauties of cohabiting with a cat?

Cats, like us, tend to be enigmatic, to appear complex. Unless
a cat is demanding food, a treat, or a lap, it is often difficult to tell
exactly what he wants or what she is thinking. And, therefore, for
those of us who dwell in the realm of nuance and empathy, cats
are perfect counterparts. We can project what we will onto
them, and who's to say that we're not right?

🐾

Cyrus has a way of sleeping, one arm—foreleg if you prefer—
under and supporting his chin, the other resting on my arm. He
curls up within the warmth of my crooked arm, but not leaning

on it. Just one paw, that right forepaw, rests on my forearm, its dark leather pad cool against my skin. Is this a gesture of affection? Is he reassuring himself that I'm still here? That's how I would construe it if our roles were reversed. That's often how I wake to find myself—one arm outstretched to touch my husband, or sometimes my cat. Or is this purely physical, a sign that I am providing desired body heat, my arm warming his cool underfoot, or that I am simply in the path of his comfort, a convenient pillow of the moment? I may never know for sure. But when I hear the low purr that lets me know he's at least partly awake, and then the rhythmic rumble quiets as he settles into a deeper sleep, these questions cease to matter. Cyrus shares that mastery that all cats have—the ability to find perfect comfort, to relax into total ease. And he's done it once more, with my love and devotion upholstering his nap, if not his dreams.

3

HOUSEHOLD GODS

When I named my kitten Cyrus, I wasn't thinking only of the historical origins of this proud and regal name. There was the sound: Cyrus begins and ends with a sibilant, the hissing *s* that cats supposedly hear better than other consonants, reminiscent as it is of the rustle of prey in the grass, or the scratching footsteps of a rodent in the walls. Plus, I liked the way it looked, and since it had also been the name of a guitarist I knew back in college, a bright guy who was something of a sophisticate, it seemed a good name, smart and healthy. Appropriately catlike. And, yes, it also came with a history that seemed right for a creature who was clearly destined for magnificence. The original Cyrus, founder of the Persian Empire, was called "the Great." The leader of the ancient Persians from roughly 550 to 529 B.C.—and my cat with his long coat was clearly part Persian himself—he conquered much of what was then the known world. More or less tolerant of the religious minorities in his realm (primarily the Jews), he was also known for his wisdom and his legal sense, which may be where one of my Cyrus's many private appellations, "attorney at law," came from. Plus, despite the dynasty he founded (well, we'll skip that one on our end), he was probably only part Persian himself, coming from a Median family. I knew my Cyrus's mother had some Siamese in her: this was clear from her markings and those on some of her other kittens, as well as in their vocal ability. I didn't think the Medes had anything to do with Siam, but it was close enough to count. And besides, in the tradition of T. S. Eliot's *Old Possum's Book of Practical Cats*, I believe in giving such regal creatures grand names.

That cats have long been recognized for their innate majesty is apparent in even a casual study of our lore and mythology. Every cat lover knows of Bastet, for example, the ancient Egyptian cat-headed goddess who oversaw both the domestic and the divine, aiding with issues of fertility as well as communicating with the dead. My diminutive male emperor aside, most such associations between the divine and the feline are, like Bastet, female, giving credence to the affiliation between us and our cats throughout humanity's history. Such associations can be found nearly the world over and date back to our earliest memories. Back to a time when women had power, real power. Goddess power.

The origins of the linkage are as basic, as primal as the life processes we controlled. In our species' early history—say the later Paleolithic days of 30,000 to 22,000 years ago—women commanded awe and respect because we controlled the original mystery. We alone, or so it seemed in those prescientific days, had the ability to reproduce. We bled and we bore children, and before humanity figured out the male's role in this, we alone seemed to have any say in the matter. When humanity, huddled and cold in a big lonely world, looked for something bigger than itself to hold off the night, it envisioned a Great Mother Goddess. Fertile, with pendulous breasts and big belly, her image has been found carved in stone throughout Northern Europe and the Mediterranean, her most feminine attributes—that belly, those breasts—symbolizing an admirable fecundity. As we see in the big-bottomed Venus of Willendorf, in the enigmatic beauties of the Cyclades, sisters had the power. The cats were soon to follow.

Somewhere along the line, smart species that we are, we invented symbolism—the substitution of one item for another—and soon our relatively slow and ponderous birth process was being wishfully compared with the relative ease and productivity of other animals, of birds and pigs and, of course, of cats. Want to show that a woman, a goddess, controls fertility? Place her by an animal that bears litters of live young: three, four, six at a time! Is it any coincidence that a statue surfaced at Catal Huyuk, in Anatolia, of a woman giving birth, supported by two great cats? Whether she is a primal Mother Goddess on a lion throne as some theorize, or simply a mortal in leopard-aided labor, the piece, which may date back to 6000 B.C. is striking. By 2500 B.C., the linkage was obvious. Then, in the great Sumerian civilization that would eventually blend into the Babylonian empire, texts were written to a high goddess called Inanna, also known as the Great Mother or Labbatu (lioness) in the two hundred or so hymns and proverbs that have survived. She's a multifaceted goddess, a woman of great power who rides a chariot pulled by lions and is often seated on a lion throne. Overseeing life and often death as well, she prefigured many of the female deities and religious figures who would follow, including—at least according to contemporary goddess theorists—the Christian Virgin Mary. Mary is not likely to be pictured with a lion under her foot, as Inanna was, but they share many of the same gifts of mercy and renewal.

Being neighbors—Sumeria and Egypt shared trade routes if not cups of sugar—Inanna most likely had some exchange with one of the other great goddesses of ancient times, Isis. Worshiped as the queen of heaven, earth, and the underworld from around 3000 B.C. through Roman times, Isis was an all-purpose goddess, overseeing life, death, writing, bread, and beer, among other divine gifts. It's no wonder that among her skills was the ability to assume the form of a cat. Her pantheon in general had a good deal of feline-divine interaction, including the lion-headed Sekhmet, a fairly ferocious goddess who warded off evil spirits (among her other duties) and her more domestic counterpart, Bastet. From 2000 B.C. onward, the cat had become the accepted symbol for this much loved goddess (who was sometimes simply called Bast), and her main temple drew throngs of worshipers to her city, Bubastis. Roughly five hundred years before domestic cats seemed to have become common, Bastet was a major player: protector and symbol of grace and love, motherhood and fertility. On the thousands of statues and inscriptions that survive, Bastet wears a cat's head, a proud large-eared feline face, perched atop a regal, commanding female torso.

Even apart from the enduring appeal of Isis and Bastet, the cat-goddess connection remained up through Greco-Roman times. By then, the Great Mother Goddess had become known as the Lady of the Beasts. You can see her still, in the gardens of the Villa d'Este outside Rome: granted, here she has taken the name of Artemis of Ephesus, usually known as the virgin huntress, which if it's not a mislabeling is at best a misnomer. As portrayed in this sixteenth-century copy of a second-century original, her body reveals the animal connection, the respect for a particularly female fecundity, because all along her belly, from her chest down to her waist, are breasts. Like a cat, she has teats lined up waiting to nourish her children. She is a goddess, a divinity who celebrates our most animal nature, which is also our most female nature and our most powerful one.

Although the cat-goddess associations of Egypt and Sumeria may be the best documented of the ancient world, traces of the same mystery may be found around the globe. In the Olmec civilization of eastern Mexico, for example, jaguars were associated with fertility four thousand years ago. In Scandinavia, the goddess Freya, who (like an early Bergman) controlled love and death, rode a chariot drawn by black cats. The Greek sphinx, unlike her Egyptian cousin, had a woman's head atop its feline body, and often donned Athena's helmet in her role as spiritual protector.

But what of Heracles and the Nemean lion, whose hide and head he always wore? Or the leopard pelts that conferred power and strength on the Aztec kings? Aren't these associations designed to link the great cats with a distinctly masculine type of power?

Yes, such associations do exist, throughout the world and throughout history. We have the recurring images of Heracles, wearing a skin wrested from the lion he throttled bare-handed. We have the 507 B.C. rendering of Egypt's King Amenemhet III as a lion-maned sphinx, and the half-jaguar ancestors who populate the mythology of the Olmec royals. But although these kings, these warriors, derive their fashion statements (and the implication of strength) from the big cats and model themselves on feline stature and dignity, it is interesting to note how this transfer—this absorption of feline properties—comes about.

These men, all of them, gain their cat goodness by conquering or killing the animals they model themselves on. The cat, in their worldviews, is the creature to be overcome. We women, however, do not have to overpower our feline counterparts; we become one with them. While the god Shiva, in Hindu lore, conquers the tiger sent to destroy him and then wears its skin, the equally fierce goddess Durga rides a tiger into battle. Overwhelmingly, we are associated with the animals themselves, and gain their qualities by this much closer, more benign relationship.

That relationship would grow increasingly complex. As civilization became subtler, our fertility grew to be associated with more than birth. Our mystery came to assume the mantle of lore, or wisdom, and of magic. Some of this can be traced in a very rough fashion along the lines of our cultural development as male and female roles diverged in the millennia building up to the great pyramids.

Theoretically, we were a fairly communal species in our hunting and gathering days, although men probably bore the brunt of the hunt. But as hunting and gathering gave way to agriculture in our Neolithic days, women—as the main gatherers—became more involved with the time-consuming work of cultivating food. The parallelism undoubtedly caught someone's eye, and a little sympathetic magic was probably hoped for as we fertile, cyclical creatures took charge of the planting and harvesting while the men monopolized killing. Perhaps more to the point, some anthropologists argue, we may have been connected to plant lore because of our direct involvement in childbirth. Women who could provide better food had more surviving offspring. Women, these theories also suggest, were the first to discover and develop the use of herbs to kill pain and staunch bleeding. Because these skills were tied in with the mystery of childbirth, their use came to seem not just a valuable but natural contribution to life's processes, but something larger and more powerful than nature. We grew apart; we inspired awe. As women gathered for childbearing, as women separated from the mingled society during their infertile time of menstruation, as women came together when age diminished their ability to conceive and bear children, our power grew in men's eyes. Somewhere along the line, our mystery grew into science and medicine. Our mystery became magic.

You can see the more developed idealization (or idolization) of women's specialities in classical mythology. The great Eleusinian mysteries of Greece, for example, were based upon the myth of Persephone. The story is simple: Persephone, the daughter of Demeter, is kidnapped by Hades and taken into the underworld. In mourning, Demeter withdraws from the world, which causes the first infertile period—the first winter. After some complex negotiation, which involves whether or not Persephone has eaten anything while with Hades (clearly a metaphor for sexual intimacy), a compromise is worked out. Persephone will spend part of the year underground with her new consort, and winter will rule. The rest of the year she will return to her loving mother, and the earth will be fertile and blooming. Sexuality and agriculture were all bound together in lovely metaphor, and the whole further abstracted into grand, high rituals that linked women with the great mysteries of life. We were a religion, and the cat was our symbol of choice.

It was no accident that Egyptians were probably the first to domesticate the cat, and probably began breeding the ancient African wild cat, *Felis silvestris libyca*, and maybe its European cousin, *Felis silvestris silvestris*, into something a tad more useful around the house as early as 6000 B.C. A rural society that grew rich on the abundant harvest from its rich silt-flooded lands, Egypt relied on grain for its greatness. Grain fed the slaves who built the pyramids. Grain fed the scholars who flocked from other Mediterranean countries to help make the library at Alexandria the largest, most comprehensive store of knowledge in the ancient world. Grain more than the giant granite monuments we now associate with its powerful dynasties made Egypt a world power. But all Pharaoh's armies could not protect grain against the smallest, most insistent thieves. If the enemy of any rural, grain-storing society is the mouse, then it stands to reason that the hero would be the cat and, to a lesser extent perhaps, the snake, which in its nonpoisonous form is equally beneficial to humans, consuming rodents enthusiastically. Perhaps these shared roles explain why the two animals were so often paired in Egyptian religious beliefs, and why cats were credited with the power to cure the bite of the asp.

Partly for such practical reasons, cats were held in high esteem in Egypt from early on. The killing of one was long considered a capital crime. The death of one, as many of us can relate to, threw families into mourning, and thousands of small feline mummies have revealed the honor in which these diminutive carnivores were held. (It should be noted here that some Egyptologists believe that many of these mummies were ritually sacrificed by priests, probably to honor cat-associated deities: an example of good intentions gone awry.)

Even later in Egypt's history, when patriarchal religions gained hold, Bastet retained much of her power, becoming the feminine counterpart of the lion-headed sun god Ra. (Incidentally, about this time the serpent became a symbol of darkness, which Ra—in his cat form—would slay each morning. A good role for the cat, who gets to be the hero, but the story once again reveals a masculine unease with mystery, darkness, and the dual nature of life.) As the roles became stratified, somewhere at the root of all their empire building, the Egyptians remained a practical people. By elevating the image of the cat, and often of the shared aspects of women and cats, they recognized where their thanks, if not their devotions, were due. For these people, the divinity of cats was not mere metaphor. For them, the cat was a practical blessing, an everyday savior in neat, brown fur.

❧

Today we are operating on the other side of the myths. We have no pressing reasons to make gods of our household companions, having instead recourse to more modern storage facilities, mouse traps, and exterminators. What we are suffering from instead, and from which our cats rescue us, is a spiritual void, a lack of mystery in the old, high sense. For too many of us, organized religion does not suffice. Yes, we may attend church or buy our tickets for the high holy days, but not enough of the incense of divinity seeps into our everyday life. What there is tends to be alienating: As active and equal participants in our workplaces and personal lives, we question the blatant paternalism of too many institutionalized forms of worship, of hierarchies upheld in dead languages. As well, too many attempts to make our faiths relevant have backfired. As campfire singalongs replace hymns, the magic that once graced our services has been colloquialized into mundanity. The god who lived in the details has been simplified out of existence.

Certainly, this loss is not felt by everyone. Many families, particularly those following more traditional lifestyles, continue to find solace and joy in the old forms. Many older people and others who still follow through with the weekly or daily rituals for various reasons—stronger cultural identification, greater vested interest in the social status quo—do find in these practices a connection with generations past or some greater sense of purpose. These people probably do not look for divinity in their pets. But for a variety of social and economic reasons, these groups are also less likely to include the majority of contemporary women. Indeed, for a great number of us the realities of our lives seem to be outside the strictures of these more traditional groups. For those of us who work and support ourselves, who live alone, or who are forging nontraditional definitions of family in couples or parenting children alone or with same-sex partners, the old rules seem no longer to apply. How likely, then, are we to find acceptance, not to mention fulfillment, in the religions of our grandparents? No surprise then that contemporary women are overwhelmingly seeking new paradigms, are digging into old religions, are finding the divine in our own homes, exploring neopagan and Eastern practices and personal faiths of our own devising.

Does this seem counterintuitive? Does it seem that those of us who try to live according to reasonable, rational, or equitable rules should not need the superstition of faith? As I write this, a three-quarter moon passes out of deep cumulus clouds and shines haloed by light reflected off the high, thin, drifting clouds of an autumn night. I understand the atmospherics involved; sunlight has bounced off the rocky lunar surface and is being refracted again through the water and ice high in our atmosphere. I accept the role of timing, of the sunset and the monthly calendar. But what I see is beautiful and beyond my reach. I cannot help watching, although I know how this satellite will make its slow progress through the tree branches. It does not need my vigilance, but I am getting something from my actions, from my devotion.

Call it psychology, then, or spirituality; the search for a greater context appears to be a constant in our species. The point is beyond simple understanding: Yes, we need symbols to understand that which is bigger than ourselves. But we need them, not only to make the mystery smaller and more digestible, but because we need to be in touch with the magic. We need to find the mystery in our everyday life, no matter how frightening this unknowable truth may be. This hunger may be part of what Carl Jung called our collective unconscious, a primitive but undeniable shared sense of imagery and understanding that helps us make sense of the unknowable, of death and oblivion and love and sex.

Perhaps we even need to feel fear: In his exploration of the *anima*, the unconscious, feminine-associated force that drives both creativity and madness, Jung wrote of the Kore, a Demeter figure who is simultaneously mother and maiden. A figure representing the often frightening duality of nature—the blood of birth as well as death, the underworld of sexuality—she often manifests herself in dreams as an animal, a cat or snake or bear. She embodies the hunter and the nurturing mother, beauty and terror, and even as she repels people—particularly men—she draws them beyond their understanding. How could she not? As the works of mythology scholar Joseph Campbell seek to show, throughout all our civilizations we have experienced this need for something greater than ourselves, no matter how frightening that greater whole may be. We need to worship and to seek and to belong to an encompassing system larger than the one we see, no matter how it makes us tremble. We need to feel awe, and are ultimately comforted by it. We need our household gods.

Wicca, the earth-based religion that has been created out of a composite of ancient practices, seeks to address some of that need. Incorporating the respect and sense of balance that have also come into Western New Age beliefs from European paganism, Native American writings, and, perhaps, from such Eastern traditions as Taoism and Buddhism, Wicca teaches respect for all life. "Do what ye will an it harm none," runs the basic precept of the religion, which was popularized—if not created—in the early twentieth century by the British witch Gerald Gardner. Although honoring the great goddess, especially in her manifestation as the earth or environment, is essential to Wiccans, there is nothing specific in the contemporary religion about cats or any animals. However, many of its practitioners, a large number of whom are female urban professionals, have adopted the idea of the companion animal. Often, although not exclusively, that animal—that familiar or spiritual guide, if you will—is a cat.

To Peg, a contemporary Wiccan and film critic, familiars are very different from pets. "A familiar is not necessarily the animal you're closest to," she explains. That honor in her household would go to Ziggy, her twelve-year-old gray-and-white tabby. The big, floppy Ziggy, she says, is her best pet, her cuddliest kitty. A familiar, she outlines the difference, serves another purpose entirely. A familar serves as a "go-between," she says, communicating between worlds or spiritual levels with his or her person.

Of the five cats with whom the critic currently cohabits, the peach-and-gray Trivia comes closest to fulfilling this magical role. Although Ziggy is the kitty Peg goes to for hugs, Trivia speaks to her soul. (The name, by the way, comes from the Latin *tri via*, meaning three roads, and not the contemporary word signifying insignificant things, Peg explains. In ancient Rome, when three roads came together, the resulting crossroad was sacred to the goddess Hecate, who controlled sorcery and creativity. The spiritual mother of witchcraft, Hecate—or Hekate—was not one to trifle with.)

What Trivia has that Ziggy lacks, Peg explains, is a sense of the world around her. Particularly notable about the smaller part-Siamese, says Peg, is her uncanny ability to tune into people's emotions, as well as into the energy of various forces around her. "Even when she was a kitten she'd look right into my eyes and know what I was thinking," says Peg of the stray a friend found in the snow nearly ten years ago.

"She's not a real cuddly cat, but she just seems to be in tune and know what I'm thinking. You know how you sense that someone's watching you? I'll have a moment like that and I'll look up and Trivia will be watching me. Whenever I look up with that odd feeling, she's the one that's there.

"She's probably an old soul," concludes Peg. "Even though Ziggy is my best friend, I've had more of a spiritual connection with Trivia."

For Dove, a fellow Wiccan, the companionship of Pounce de Lion, her six-year-old orange tabby, underscores the basic tenets of her faith. "I believe cats are psychic," says the Ohio-based student. "And if anything can help you lose your ego and be at one with the universe, it's a pet." She begins to list the ways our relationships with our cats encourage us into selflessness, enumerating the lengths we go to in order to feed, comfort, and pamper them. Fulfilling such duties, she explains, can help us get in touch with forces beyond our daily lives.

"Being able to love this fuzzy face, that's sometimes so precious and tiny and other times just a fat cat . . ." she trails off as Pounce saunters by, curious about the conversation. "When you clean a litter box, that's got to be love. You tolerate their mistakes, to a point, and hopefully they'll tolerate yours. It's a relationship, and there's no way you cannot have a spiritual link with someone you love that much.

"It's like having a 'significant other,' but it's a fur ball and not another human. The communication is sometimes trying because you can't always be clear. But she intuitively knows what to do."

Respect for the boundaries in that relationship keeps Dove from incorporating Pounce into her Wiccan rituals, called circles, a restraint that Peg shows as well. "She's a different species," explains Dove. "Any spirituality she has may be different from mine."

Which is not to say that Pounce doesn't sometimes seem to take an interest in Dove's nightly rituals, when she draws a circle in the air to define a sacred space—a sort of natural sanctuary—to be filled with candles and chants. "When I do circles, she's there," she says, referring to the magical space that serves, in a meditative way, to help her find a deeper peace. "Once in a while, she might walk up and rub against the altar. But if it were a daytime ritual, she wouldn't be there. She'd be looking out the window."

For these women, as for many of us, the goddess remains central to life. "My cat," says Dove, "in many ways is nurturing me."

Despite their reverence for cats—and for all life—these contemporary Wiccans remain in the minority. That doesn't mean that the divine, mystical cat-woman linkage has disappeared from the mainstream, however. Although cats in our civilization are, since the Victorian era, more likely to be house pets (a tradition, like so much of higher culture, adopted from the Chinese who for centuries appreciated such pets), they still retain that air of mystery. Like so much of our past that has become fodder for popular culture, the association with women and sexuality remains as well. Our conjoined traits of fertility and cleverness, sexuality and magical longevity pop up everywhere, from literature to the funny pages. Consider, for a moment,

Krazy Kat: love-crazed and unshakable, this 1913 creation spends her life mooning for the affections of one Ignatz, a mouse. (Some comics experts will also note that at times Krazy is referred to as "he"; however, the openness of the Kat's passion and large neck bow seem to justify this writer's opinion of the komic kitty as more or less female.) But while she is a figure of ridicule—hence the humor—she is also amazingly tough. Her amorous spirit never falters, and she constantly survives tossed bricks, epitomizing the cat's legendary nine lives. (That number, by the way, has many possible derivations. As three times three, it's a important sign in numerology. Stories link it to various magical counts, including the number of times the prophet Muhammad stroked his cat Muezza when the cat thanked the prophet for his graciousness. Muhammad had cut off his sleeve rather than disturb Muezza, who had been sleeping on the soft fabric.)

The same traits surfaced in 1916, in "Archy and Mehitabel," the subtler creation of *New York Sun* columnist Don Marquis (and also notably illustrated by Krazy Kat creator George Herriman). In these serialized poetic adventures, the perpetually amorous female is cast as a life-hardened alley cat, the street-toughened Mehitabel. "Wotthehell," she responds to life's knocks, as recorded by Marquis's male alter-ego, the cockroach Archy, into whom the soul of a poet has transmigrated. "Wotthehell," she says after each sexual adventure—with a dashing French tom cat or a poetically inclined stray—comes to a close. Unscrupulous and, perhaps to the bug, dangerous (a point we will touch on later), the not-quite-a-lady cat remains an object of fascination to the insect poet. Admiring her, as his predecessors did their deities, he presents her as a creature of style. *"Toujours gai,"* she tells her bug friend, is her motto. Mehitabel may be rough around the edges, a tad haggard and with one game leg, but she's a goddess. *"Toujours gai,"* she sings. "There's life in the old dame yet."

In the hands, hearts, and minds of women artists, cats take on a wider range of meaning. Diane White, for example, spent much of her career at the *Boston Globe* writing a column that often centered on the adventures of "Killer," the nom de plume of her nineteen-year-old spotted big boy, Rossi. Alone of her two cats (the other being the massively muscular Robby), Rossi found fame and an adoring audience who followed his adventures with vets, furniture, and occasionally Diane's other obsessions—all under a pseudonym that protected the huge altered tom's privacy. "We almost named him that, actually," says Diane, laughing, as we sit and watch the creaky old cat trek into the room. "Killer! It just seemed to fit."

Rossi's hunting days are over, and Diane no longer writes the biweekly feature, but something from those columns has remained in the collective unconscious. "I still get letters asking how he is," she notes, as Rossi surveys the room. The last few dealt with his aging, with his kidney problems and weight loss, and I can understand why readers are concerned. For Diane, however, those columns were a celebration of a relationship. "I always loved writing about him," says the comfortably built blonde, who has settled into her own chair. "I find cats endlessly fascinating.

"People who didn't like cats were baffled by it," she adds, and we share our memories of one particular editor who was clearly not a pet lover. "Why would I waste my time and this valuable space writing about my cat?" She remembers his frequent complaints. Her column outlasted his tenure.

Still, she isn't completely sure what the appeal was in the week in, week out portrayals of "Killer's" adventures and mishaps. "Maybe I anthropomorphize him too much," she says, looking over at the pacing cat. "But it always seemed to me that when I was writing about him I was writing about myself. It always seemed to me that he got the better of me in our relationship and for some reason that always seemed very symbolic." Rossi looks up and considers Diane's lap, then settles on the couch beside me and curls up to sleep.

Fans of the New York jazz scene have had a similarly intimate relationship with a feline named Arnold. Like his caretaker and mentor, composer Karen Mantler, the big burly tom graced recordings and concerts in the downtown circuit before his demise in 1991 at the age of twenty-four.

"He was really my brother," says Karen of the beefy tuxedo cat who showed up at her family's Woodstock, New York, home one morning when she was about eight. "I grew up with him."

Because she also grew up as the daughter of musicians Carla Bley and Michael Mantler, singing on her mother's records at the age of five, Karen naturally gravitated toward music. Arnold's debut came later, when Karen was studying composition at the Berklee College of Music in Boston. "I was trying to write something and I was having problems," says the honey-blonde New Yorker with her mother's pouty lips. "I called my mom and she said, 'Try writing about something you really love.'" Arnold was back home at the time, living with Bley and her partner, Steve Swallow, but his image revved up Karen's creative jets. The music, she says, "just flowed out of me."

The result, "My Cat Arnold," links her cool, spare sound to the kind of warm words that any cat owner could love. "Arnold . . . more than a cat!" she sings on the 1989 recording of the same name, following the tune picked out on her keyboards. "Big furry pillow with claws."

"I wasn't going to keep the words," she remembers, twelve years after that song became the title track of her first solo album. "I was just using the words to help shape the tune. I thought they were too personal and silly."

Something clicked, however, and the twenty-plus-pound "pillow" continued as Karen's muse. "It was the beginning of the whole process of songwriting. When I write, I have to think about something I really care about. It has to come from somewhere really deep and solid within me.

"I started taping him," she says, explaining the vociferous morning ritual that made such sampling easy. "He had a very regular schedule and each morning he'd go to wake my mother. He'd go through a whole range of emotions—from a really happy 'Good morning' through a sad 'I'm really hungry' to 'Oh! I'm starving!' He would just let them roar."

Arnold made a guest appearance on her follow-up recording, *Karen Mantler and Her Cat Arnold Get the Flu*, his distinctively articulated morning meow joining a chorus of voices on "The Flu." He became a regular part of her concerts, as well, thanks to that home taping, and developed a following of his own.

When Arnold died on Karen's birthday in 1991 while she was cat-sitting for her touring mother, she went through her tapes to give him a final solo. The resulting blues interlude forms the centerpiece of her requiem, "Arnold's Dead," on the album *Farewell*. Although her latest recording, *Pet Projects*, mulls over the possibility of another companion, she has yet to find a replacement for Arnold, in the studio or in her heart.

"He was the most loving cat," she says, remembering when he showed up fully grown at their isolated country house. The family had tried to keep him out, figuring that such a well-fed, well-mannered gentleman must belong to someone. But Arnold kept coming back until they relented. "He wanted to be held. He'd put his paws around your neck and bury his nose in your ear. It seemed he could speak. He understood us.

"He was involved in music a lot," recalls Karen, looking back on Arnold's oeuvre. Although his work was primarily impromptu, the studio in the basement of Bley's house afforded the big cat ample creative opportunities. "Carla would be writing music and he would jump on the piano and try to interrupt. He was always down there in the studio, getting in trouble, lying on the console.

"He hated saxophones. He would run from the studio when there were saxes," remembers Karen. "Otherwise, he liked everything."

Cats, with their graceful beauty, have appeared in women's visual arts throughout history. Contented as the Gwen John's kitty sleeping in the British Museum or transgressive, as in filmmaker Carolee Schneeman's nude *Infinity Kisses, 1981–87,* which depicted embraces shared with her kitty Vesper, these portraits establish iconic images and tear them down again, always engaging viewers with their power.

At times, however, cats may inspire art without inhabiting it. No felines, for example, can be found among the icons in Cynthia Von Buhler's household. Other art hangs there in abundance: cool, detached portraits that evoke figures of history and literature; tall, glossy collages that combine religious imagery with the more modern symbolism of commercialism—the saint and the household cleanser; the self-portrait and the meat-packing diagram. On almost every wall of the large, dark Victorian Cynthia shares with her husband, Adam, one of her paintings or collages beckon; the walls themselves are painted a rich, deep red, providing the dramatic setting her disturbing images require.

"Being an artist is selfish," she says, lounging in the living room with a few of her eight cats. "Sometimes I think I should do something better with my life. I should save cats."

In addition to her painting, Cynthia has already done quite a bit of feline rescue. All her cats—from the eldest, fifteen-year-old Cleo, to the still-kittenish Mr. Pacman—were originally strays. Mr. Pacman was brought to her after being hit by a car: after several hundred dollars of surgery the rangy adolescent, black with knee-high white booties, still walks with a limp, his left hind leg turned slightly outward as he scampers around us. Some of the cats that make their home in this museumlike space are still almost feral. Although she adopted the Fuzzy Pumper, a black longhair, as a kitten, he will only tolerate Cynthia and Adam's presence. I have heard of his pale green eyes and his motherly grooming behavior—he insists on licking all his fellow cats—but he does not show at all during our talk.

Cynthia's house is not a place for feline rivalries. Allowances are made for old favorites; Cleo spends most of her time sequestered in the upstairs gallery space. Other cats have been adopted out to more suitable homes. With a string of friends and acquaintances that have grown along with Cynthia's career, she can usually find a place for every cat. "There's always someone who wants a pet," she says. Mussolini, who won renown for eating mice whole, now enjoys being the only cat of an elderly woman who adores him. The spoiled Taj, a white Angora whose original owner had passed away, has also moved on to single-cat status.

"If we do keep this house, maybe I should make it into a shelter for cats," Cynthia continues. She and Adam have no plans to have children, she confides, and therefore must only budget for the two hundred dollars a month or so she spends on cat food and litter. Thus far, all the cats she has fostered or adopted have come from her own urban neighborhood, where the heavy student population means a lot of abandoned pets. Not that her concern is strictly local. She recounts the plight of stray cats in Israel. "There were cats just giving birth on the side of the road, and people were saying, 'They're just like rats! Kill them!'

"I should go around the world rescuing cats," she says, returning to her original idea. "It would be noble."

Being an artist, we agree, necessitates a certain amount of self-involvement. On the most basic level, in order to write or to paint, one must decide that the work is worth the time. One must say, "My creative ideas have more value than my labors at a job. Or than my cleaning the kitchen." It is satisfying, we conclude, but at times it seems both futile and vain.

"I'm not happy," says Cynthia. "I'm always wanting something." We discuss Buddha, or perhaps it's John Ruskin, on the subject of peace and freedom from desire. When we look at the two cats who have joined us, Mr. Pacman now purring like an engine stretched out along my thigh and Cowie's Baby sleeping on the sofa, her white monkey face blissfully at ease, we seem to have a model for perfect peace.

"Aren't they beautiful?" Cynthia asks. "I want to honor them," she says, outlining the latest series of children's stories she is writing. These stories will incorporate her cats, most notably Olympus, who died on the way to the vet a month before of a cancer that appeared out of nowhere and was hidden for too long under his lush fur.

Olympus was not an easy cat to care for. He had been one of her ferals, like the large, spotted white Mr. Stoic, who now sleeps curled on the porch inside the heated cat house Cynthia and Adam provide for their less well-socialized felines. Olympus had been wary, although hungry, and Cynthia had fed him for four years before he finally allowed himself to be taken in. "I can still remember him lying on the porch, totally happy. At least we gave him a few years of happiness."

Olympus inspired one of her new stories, about a cat who refuses to come in. More of them though, she acknowledges, are really about herself. She tells me about one, "Tabby and Fancy," that records a conversation between a happy feral and a discontented house cat. There's no question which role Cynthia assumes. "I almost never have fun. I'm always thinking I've got to work. I should," she pauses, "be happier than I am."

Feet tucked up beneath her, the artist looks perfectly content, particularly when Mr. Pacman, roused from his nap, climbs up on her shoulder, his black fur almost matching her dark hair. His image, she says, is not one that will likely make its way into her paintings, nor will the faces of any of her cats.

"Those portraits?" she asks, looking around at the antique frames, the solemn, sainted faces that stare down at us. "A lot of those portraits are really negative," she explains. "And I don't have negative emotions about my cats. I don't have those feelings that I need to get out."

Sometimes, in other words, our cats inspire us simply by their presence. Some mysteries are best left to the dark.

4

WHEN THE FUR FLEW

Although I don't like to admit it, a former co-worker of mine may have prompted me to write this book. He was a lonely single guy, and although he and I did not often see eye to eye, I do remember trying to fix him up with a single female friend of mine, the way we coupled women tend to do, thinking, "One woman's office burr could be another's dreamboat. It's worth a try." Foolish, right? Anyway, as I was telling him about her, warning him of her less than perfect figure (and he no Olympic diver), praising her creativity, the big heart that had kept us friends for years, I found myself telling him about her pets. Specifically her two cats. "Oh no," he interrupted me. "No thank you. Not another single woman with cats."

"Not another single woman with cats." That was all he needed to say. I knew, as we all probably know, exactly what he meant. With one short denial he had signified a rejection of a huge group of women, a group that had included at some point myself and most of my female friends. And although I readied myself, in

my office geisha mode, to listen to his reasons with a smile and to offer my counterarguments in a pleasant tone—*to listen to one more man list one more time the rationalizations of why a woman who loves a cat would never be loved by him*—I found my gorge rising.

There were several reasons for this. First, even as I prepared to do it, I resented shilling my friend. She was—she is—a fine woman. A better woman than he deserved and probably a better human being on almost any scale, barring a testosterone count, than he could ever be. Who was I to apologize for her womanly hips? Her mature belly, indicative of sensual tastes that he would never appreciate? And, of course, as I bowed to his rejection, accepting without argument his brush-off, I realized that I was, in a way, agreeing with his judgment of us, accepting without questioning the idea that a woman with a cat, particularly a woman with a cat and without a man, was somehow embarrassing or lacking or immature. Here he was, feeling free to put down women like me and my friends without even explaining his gross and broadly drawn prejudice, and I was buying into it. Finally, belatedly, I began to wonder why. They never met, at least not through me. But this book, in part, came from my own thoughts about why they never should.

What do we think of when we hear of that pairing, woman and cat, and why does it so often raise a sneer? We enjoy the comfort of the warm couch companion, the easy acceptance of the feline presence. We refer to our kitties, our dear pets, in affectionate terms. We admire their sensuality, their beauty, their seemingly intuitive and self-determined natures—all traits we would like to strengthen in ourselves. If anything, our ability to love and nurture a pet bodes well for our capacity to care for other living creatures. In this light, cats seem a natural complement to our femininity, part of our mystique.

And yet we all acknowledge the negative stereotypes that

accompany this relationship. We wince and apologize. "I'm not one of those women who goes crazy over her cats," a good friend said to me over lunch not long ago. "I've got a sense of perspective." She was telling me this after relating her recent experience with an animal communicator, aka a cat psychic, and before passing along some info gleaned on a cat lovers' Web site, a demonstration of denial that made me smile. Clearly, by most standards my cat-loving buddy would be described by many as just what she had declared herself not to be: cat obsessed. Another "single woman gone nutty over her cats." If I may use the term: pussy whipped.

There it is again, that negative feline-female connotation—and yes, I realize that this particular gynophobic term typically refers to domination of a man by a woman, at least originally through sexual control. But even those of us who have grown comfortable with the term *pussy* for our genital area and have come to embrace it in self-defense (and as so much more friendly than its slang equivalent, cunt) have to wonder. Where is all the hatred coming from?

It's been around long enough to have become part of our folklore: Old wives' tales credit cats with murderous instincts, saying, for example, that they suck the breath out of newborn babies. More contemporary detractors are usually more discreet, accusing felines instead of overweening self-interest. If they purr and come to you, it is because they want to be fed. If they climb into your lap, it is to ensure your affection for the next feeding.

These thoughts ran through my head the morning after Thanksgiving when I awoke to find one arm freezing, except for the area where Cyrus was leaning up against me, purring loudly enough to wake me. I soon realized he had his reasons. The night before, glutted with turkey and stuffing, I had gone to sleep without noticing that the heat had gone out. Cyrus had had his fill, as well, but not being under a down comforter, he had become aware of the plummeting mercury earlier than I did and curled up in the crook of my arm. "He wants my warmth," I thought, though my heart was touched by his hearty purr and the soft weight of him all along my upper arm. "And I don't blame him."

Cyrus has long had the habit of sleeping by my side. At some point each night, he usually jumps onto the bed, kneads my arm, and lies down beside me. Sometimes he rests his chin on my arm or on my hand, sometimes one paw, and sometimes he leans his whole considerable upper-body weight against my wrist. The custom had grown so strong over the years that I regularly fall asleep on my back now, with my left arm above the covers, slightly crooked to offer him proper access.

What was different this morning was the way he leaned into me, the completeness with which he had tucked almost every inch of himself against me, his butt against my side, his back wedged into my armpit, and his shoulders and head lined up against my arm. This was more than affection, I thought. This is how the pride survives winter, if winter on the Serengeti ever gets as cold as New England. I called the gas company and retreated once more under the covers, this time flipping one side of the down quilt over my feline companion and my own cold arm. He purred us both back to sleep.

When cat detractors call our pets selfish, I thought to myself a few hours later when I once again awoke to the cold and, finally, the repairman, they mean it as an insult. They are implying that self-interest rules our bonds of affection, or habit, or love. In direct opposition, of course, are their ideas about humans (and usually dogs), who they believe are different, more altruistic, more emotionally motivated. I think it is this self-deception, in part, that makes me love cats all the more.

Yes, cats are selfish. So are we all. The concept of selfish altruism—that even when we aid others it is because ultimately we ourselves benefit—probably explains how we as a species have survived to cover the planet. Public works? A more complacent, socialized environment in which to live. Charity? Fewer angry, hungry people. Affection? A way to tie others to us so that they will care for us when we need them to. Maybe this sounds cynical, but I see no shame in it. We are all Darwinian creatures, and if cats are a little more open about it, so much the better.

In earlier times, of course, cats have been not merely derided as selfish: they have been seen as evil, and the women who associated with them considered the servants of the devil. For if some of the hatred we encounter is directed at our pets, much more of it is aimed at us, and has been throughout history. Such rage, predicated on fear, probably grew in direct proportion to our mysteries.

The linkage between the mystical powers of women and cats seems well established throughout time. As our dubious civilization advanced, however, those mysteries grew more complicated, and to men, more threatening. We can see the roots of this antipathy in older cultures. To be linked with the spiritual doorway of birth, for some, meant a connection with life's other great doorway: death. Creativity and destruction, we held the reins to it all. Which may explain, in part, why the Hindu goddess Durga, the destroyer, rides a tiger into battle, as well as why Hecate, who came from Asia Minor to be Rome's goddess of creativity and magic, birth and, of course, death, was eventually denigrated to the less divine and more simplistic role of evil crone, or witch.

Mythologist Nancy Hathaway has compiled quite a list of dark goddesses in her excellent book *The Friendly Guide to Mythology,* many associated with the underworld and often with cats as well, such as Yambe-akka of the Scandinavian Lapps, who required a sacrifice of black cats. Even Freya's cats—a likely precursor of the European idea of witch's cats—have been described as demonic, probably because they did her bidding. And, yes, they flew. (Some legends add that this Norse goddess of love and death had to "steal" her magic treasure by sleeping with four dwarves—a typical tie-in between women's sexuality and the male fear of cuckolding and impotence—and that her cats were rewarded for their service by transformation into witches, who would then disguise themselves as cats.) When cats were first described as having nine lives one implication was that they had the power to go into the unknown—to die that is—and then return. Scary magic by any means.

Link up our powers over birth and death and the hold our sexuality had over men and it becomes rather easy to see why we began to scare them. If one way of dealing with fear is to belittle its source, another is to demonize it, making it larger than life so that any kind of attack upon it is justifiable. By the time our Western civilization had settled into its so-called Renaissance, we had done both. The powerful woman had begun, on one hand, to be reviled as the witch and, on the other, to be trivialized by the emerging sexism that a growing bourgeoisie could afford. Since a woman's labor and knowledge was no longer quite so necessary for every family's survival, she became suspect and also financially irrelevant. She was a demon, Satan's lover. Or she was harmless to the point of witlessness: the befuddled female, or the homey figure of the grandmother (or sexless mother) every man wishes he had.

This diminishing of our power, this demonizing of it, began

before the rise of the paternalistic religions. In his *A History of Witchcraft*, Jeffrey R. Russell traces our image of the malevolent female witch back to the Sumerian Ardat-Lili, or Lilitu, a female demon who flew at night in the company of owls and lions. On her nocturnal prowls, she seduced mortal men, drank their blood, and killed children.

Not an auspicious beginning. However, with the rise of the great male gods, misogyny really took off. Some goddess-oriented historians point to the conquests of the great old civilizations of Crete and Old Europe by more primitive invaders from the steppes, those who valued male brute strength over the more communal skills of agriculture (the domination, as Riane Eisler put it, of the blade over the chalice). At a basic level, the revolution may be the natural result of humanity's growing understanding of the natural world. The great Judeo-Christian leaders—heirs of those warlike wandering tribes—surely understood the role of men in conception and birth. To some extent, they appreciated the woman's role as well, at least as a mere sexual vessel. (Although as late as the Greeks, we hear Apollo bragging, "The father can father forth without a mother," in Aeschylus's *The Eumenides*.) No matter, in the Judeo-Christian desire to replace the old religions, they seemed to feel the need to discredit the ancient icons. The mystery of the Goddess had to be thrown down. The cat and the woman had to be separated, our catlike nature excised.

The attack began on our sexuality, our most feline feature. In some versions, such as Judaism, somewhere along the line the segregation that women had probably chosen for themselves during menstruation or nearing childbirth became a punishment, a casting out. Women who were proving themselves fertile were suddenly "unclean," and so the women's tent became a place of shame, not refuge. Historians of the old religions, such as Raven Grimassi, point out that even in their imagery, the new religions tended to desexualize women, to remove the ancient source of our power. The icons that survive reflect this stripping down, as the many-teated Lady of the Beasts became the virgin mother. Our pendulous breasts and healthy bellies were whittled back into the slender, preadolescent Madonnas of Gothic iconography. We were unsexed, weakened, and made peripheral to the faiths and mysteries over which we once ruled.

Where we couldn't be trivialized, however, we had to be destroyed. And when the Lady of the Beasts, the threatening momma-goddess, could not be forced into the role of virgin or noble mother, she was cast into the relatively defenseless form of an older woman. As such, she becomes an easy scapegoat for the village woes. Crops fail? Blame a sorceress. A new husband proves impotent? Definitely a woman's curse. *Cherchez la femme*: Look for the witch.

It wasn't always such. Early Christians, according to Grimassi, were quite happy to accept the preexisting symbolism of cats as stand-ins for a healthy fertility. It was only when their fledgling religion began to be formalized into an establishment faith that they redefined, and finally rejected, a perfectly good symbol. As time went on, the religion's leaders seemed worried by their lack of control over women. In a neat switch, the felines that had stood in for our admirable powers came to symbolize the so-called evil parts of our natures, our lack of restraint, our carnality, and godlessness. Sexuality is clearly the link here, for although the most popular current depiction of the witch is as an ugly crone—a woman who, in our youth-obsessed culture, we usually regard as sexless—a rampant carnal appetite has historically been part of the witch's evil nature. Throughout the European model at peak popularity in the fifteenth and sixteenth centuries, her Sabbath festivities were, in fact, orgies that had her copulating with the Devil, who assumed an animal form. (We can't entirely blame Christians, or even Europeans, for this bias: Even among the Zande of southern Sudan, according to witchcraft historian Russell, witch cats routinely had sexual relations with women.)

It was in Europe, though, that the hatred grew deadly. Once we were demonized, we became the target of all the rage a growing, confused, and soon plague-ridden civilization could muster. By some estimates, the victims ran into the tens of thousands. We know of the Salem witch trials of 1692, which ended with twenty executions, but the killings started hundreds of years earlier. In 829, the Synod of Paris first decreed capital punishment for witches and sorcerers, with the first record of such an execution remaining from 1022, when a woman was put to death in Orleans, France. Records are scarce, but we know that Ireland had joined the European craze by 1324, when it executed Dame Alice Kyteler, and from that point on the flames grew hotter. Some historians, such as Grimassi, count in excess of fifty thousand executions in Northern Europe during the witch-burning mania that swept Europe in the fifteenth century. Women—and often cats—died, murdered by fire, by drowning, or by the weight of huge stones laid atop them. Even after the killings of women stopped, the socially, sometimes legally sanctioned killing of cats continued until contemporary times, which certainly didn't help contain the plague or other vermin-borne diseases. Indeed, England didn't officially repeal the last of its antiwitchcraft laws until 1951.

The correlation between cats, women, and evil hasn't ended with the bloodshed, as any observer of popular culture knows. Take the all-American hero, Batman, and who do we find opposing him? Catwoman, of course, a woman of infinitely more power then the wimpy Batwoman or the more enduring, and sexually immature afterthought that is Bat Girl. Catwoman is exceedingly more imposing than these do-gooders, and by making her debut in the comic-rich year of 1940, she predates them by more than a decade. (Comics historian Trina Robbins identifies the first Batwoman in 1956, the first Bat Girl in 1961.)

It is true that from her first appearance in *Batman* No. 1, Catwoman has been naughty rather than evil: Her human alter ego, Selina Kyle, is put upon and therefore has good reason for donning her cat identity. Plus, unlike some of Batman's other enemies, her crimes tend to be minor: theft of jewelry and other pretty items, or at most aiding other supervillains. She never kills.

Basically, she's very much a male fantasy creation, and epitomizes the love-hate relationship men have with our power, with the stereotypical associations between women and cats. She is sexual, and therefore she must be bad. She is an independent woman, and therefore she must be bad. In adventure after adventure, she clearly attracts Batman just as much as she does her leering male readers, and therefore she must be bad. But she must never become so terrifying as to no longer succeed as a male fantasy of forbidden fruit, or her creators would have written themselves out of a juicy character. She never fully embodies the traditional strengths of cat-associated women. She never gives off more than a frisson of fear. She is not the Panther Queen, for example, seeking to sink her fangs into human flesh, or the Lioness who would leap and kill. She is Catwoman; she can be made to purr.

Interestingly, the sexy, powerful woman of comic book greatness was not always bad nor was she always drawn with the exaggerated sexual attributes we've come to expect from the medium. In fact, The great range of such catwomen was stressed to me by a rather feline young salesclerk at my local comic-book store, a college student I soon learn was raised with anywhere from seven to twelve cats. Although she seems a strong young woman in her own right, she's too busy to chat for long about cat images. "You should talk to my mom," she says, giving me her card. "She's totally into cats." When I do, her mom laughs. "She learned her attitude from the cats," she tells me.

In the comics' first heyday, my young adviser did take the time to point out, artists—often women—created a range of female-feline characters. Miss Fury and the Black Cat, who both came to life in 1941, both donned great powers with their feline apparel: Miss Fury assumed her superstrength with a black panther's skin that happens to cover her entire body and the Black Cat—a Hollywood "stunt girl" by day—wore a nifty shorts outfit and cat-eared mask. These were heroines, rather than titillating villainesses, and fought Nazis, mad scientists, and other forces of evil in their era. Miss Fury, the senior by four months, was created by a woman, the cat-loving Tarpe Mills (who, according to historian Robbins, changed her first name from the more gender-specific June in order to aid her comic-book drawing career à la George Sand). Mills even wrote her own pet, the Persian Perri-Purr, into the strip as the feline companion of Miss Fury's alter ego, socialite Marla Drake.

Such positive identification could not survive. *Miss Fury* stopped publishing in 1952, *The Black Cat* in 1963. Since then good-girl cat-ladies have recurred occasionally, but their claws have been clipped. In the early 1960s, the Archies comic strip *Josie and the Pussycats* portrayed a trio of fun-loving gals who donned tiger-striped tails and ears to solve crimes. Beloved by many of us, but minor in a mainstream commercial sense. However, music-loving feminists should note that those girls also play in a rock band, when not fighting crime, and no matter how pop their music may have sounded to more sophisticated ears, they prefigured the young female "riot grrrls" who would claim punk music for themselves thirty years later. In 1970 when Josie first made her television appearance, first-wave feminism was ready to blossom, and this perky and adorable packaging of it was the first sight of it many of us saw.

As those of us who grew up with the counterculture know, underground comics have responded better to feminism, presenting a solid panoply of superheroines and even the occasional feline female (such as the short-lived Cat, who rode feminism's first wave from 1972 to 1973). For the most part, however, feline superheroines have been eliminated from the mainstream, replaced by the slinky sexy bad girl we know so well. As envisioned by DC Comics' Bob Kane and Bill Finger in the Batman debut, the first Catwoman already had the midnight locks, the wide-set eyes, and the full breasts that would stir superheros (and their fans) for the next sixty years. Although her costume and some peripheral details changed over the years, in response to the puritan Comics Code of the fifties and to fashion foibles, her full curves continued to reveal her as a sexually mature adult.

That image came alive in the television version of *Batman* in the person of Julie Newmar, who brought the character to the small screen in March 1966. Clad in a form-fitting costume that clearly showed off her womanly attributes, Newmar's Catwoman epitomized an aggressive, confident, and very adult sexuality in that serial show, and all its camp humor couldn't conceal her power. In fact, much of her bad-girl behavior, seen in retrospect, stems from her sexual frustration. Her repeated failure to entice the goody-two-shoes Caped Crusader provides much of the knowing laughter, and despite her comic-book heritage as a master (or mistress) thief, her chief crimes on TV are really her constant attempts to seduce our hero. (Who, it may be noted, may have had the heavy upper-body musculature of a mature male but, despite occasional waverings, still preferred to hang with his latency-period homeboy, Robin.)

Her replacement in the show's third season by the singer-actress Eartha Kitt raises some further questions about the role of female sexuality in the public eye. Some fans theorize that Kitt was brought in to make the character more adult, and more evil, in order to not compete with the "good" object of desire, Bat Girl. Kitt certainly made her Catwoman a more dangerous feline and built on her existing sex-kitten image, established in the early fifties by her sultry delivery of such songs as "C'est Si Bon" and "Santa Baby." But cultural critics must also note that the change in ethnicity—from the Caucasian Newmar to the African-American Kitt—added a new element of "otherness" to the role. Suddenly, she is not only sexual and female, she is also the only nonwhite person regularly seen on the series. Kitt countered much of the stereotyping of this role—particularly the exaggerated sexualization of African-American women—by polishing her character, making her much more the urban sophisticate than the street kitten. But for being female, being feline, being sexual—if not for being black—she was still permanently consigned to the wrong side of the series' moral.

Our more contemporary feminist reactions to the feline-female sexuality connection can be seen in the updated version of the role, the Catwoman that Michelle Pfeiffer portrayed in the 1992 film, *Batman Returns*. For here we finally find the revival of the original, featuring the much more plausible story of Selina Kyle, a revenge fantasy with which any put-upon cat-loving woman can identify. In this film, we witness the creation of the villainess out of an overlooked, overworked, and, well, mousy young thing who is pushed too hard, literally. Luckily, our heroine is not alone, as the villain who has tossed her off a roof believes. Her apparent murder has been witnessed by her many feline housemates, who love her and who bring her back to life, in part by imbuing her with their essence. When she wakes, she finds her senses more alert, her strength and flexibility increased exponentially. The Selina they revive is not a Selina who can be kept down.

We are witnessing a return to nature, a reconnection to the primal. The new Selina is angry, yes, and seeks to hurt those who have hurt her. But her anger has clued her in to other, more basic elements of herself. She ceases to hide from her womanly nature, which is also her feline nature, and instead revels in her beauty and her sexuality, as well as her strength and her anger. She has blossomed from sexless office drone to avenging lioness.

Some may argue, with reason, that Catwoman is still not a fully realized person. As anyone who has ever squeezed her curves into a formfitting costume can attest, there is a lot of male fantasy in this feline antiheroine. Catwoman is essentially a dominatrix, the kitten with a whip who will "force" men into guiltless enjoyment of the sexual abandon they have sought all along. She is, ultimately, a male creation. She is also, we should note, a comic-book character created essentially for pubescent boys who may be excited, but are certainly unnerved, by adult female sexuality.

Still, some of us feminists may admit to more than a grudging fondness for her as well. Maybe it is because she looks great in latex. But also, behind that black mask, Catwoman embodies the classic connection of cat and woman, and she can kick ass. Like her goddess ancestors, she is eternal in that time is on her side. For Batman, as for all his followers, puberty waits. But Catwoman, although she loses again and again, always returns, and even her "death" in a 1977 comic has not stilled her life in comics, graphic novels, or, clearly, film. And she is everywhere: Although the DC Comics antiheroine isn't credited, echoes of the "Feline Felon" can be seen all over pop culture: in Catherine Zeta-Jones's sexy cat burglar, complete with skintight black out-fit; pairing off contentiously with Sean Connery in *Entrapment*; as a part-cat futuristic heroine in television's *Dark Angel*; and a dozen other images in popular culture today. The implication that she will win out, that someday her good-boy foil will respond, is always present. Cats and adult female sexuality are out there, in the dark future, waiting to pounce.

5

THE SENSUAL KITTY

In parts of the Roman Empire a cat killing a bird was seen as
the female element of life assaulting the male element of
spirituality. But then cats have often figured in the battle of
the sexes, being so fecund and so willing.

—Roger Caras, *A Celebration of Cats*

Most of us don't put it so poetically. Which is not to say we
haven't experienced it.

"The last two men I lived with—before my current man who
I think was a cat in his previous life—had serious problems with
my relationships with my cats," says Michelle, who raises purebred American shorthairs. "There was a lot of, 'You love your
cats more than you love me' and, 'You can't have a relationship
with anyone but your cats.' "

"I run into those negative images all the time," agrees Emily,
who keeps company with two tabbies, Madison and Carla. "Say-

ing stuff like, 'You're going to end up alone' or, 'You're ruining all your chances.' Me and all my girlfriends are cat people, and we all laugh off the stereotypes. Frankly we prefer the company of cats to most of the boyfriends who pass through."

Given the associations between cats and women, notably our sexuality and our independence, perhaps we should not be surprised that cats often become ammunition in the battle between the genders. More than any other pet, cats evoke negative responses: antipathy and sometimes ridicule. Such reactions may come from the same men who find Catwoman sexy: When our cat natures are fantasy, they're fine. But when our real-life relationships with Monsieur le Chat or Madame Tabby intrude, the men in our lives can get vicious. Sometimes, it's simple jealousy as they compete for our time and love. Why are we paying attention to our pets instead of them? Sometimes, it's more complex: As with the witch trials of centuries past, there are elements of our essentially feline natures that they cannot control and yet they find attractive. They fear their own vulnerability in the face of these unknowns and react by blaming us—and our pets. Usually, it's just so silly. So often what these men claim to disdain they could be taking pleasure in: the sensual nature of our favorite pets.

Think about the pleasure afforded by the presence of a cat, and think about how wonderful it can make a person feel: You stroke a cat and enjoy the give of the fur, the smooth flow of hairs laid down on hairs as the pressure of your outstretched hand raises warmth and perhaps a mild vibration. He (or she), in turn, arches into the caress, elongating his already supple body to prolong the pleasure. When you stop he turns toward you, nudging you to begin again, the cool damp of his nose pushing against your hand until you lift it to where he wants it, to where it will once more make him feel oh-so-good. If it weren't for our innate avoidance of incest with something so close to us, the situation would probably get a lot trickier than it usually does. But if anything can teach us about pleasure and reciprocity, at the very least, a cat can. So what do these men dislike?

It is true that to enjoy these sensuous animals you have to be on their good side. And for many people there may be too much of a history of hostility to overcome. Sometimes, in truth, the cat has launched the first offensive. Cats, after all, have been known to be possessive of their people, perhaps even more than we are of them. Their means of relating their jealousy (or if you want to use an animal behaviorist's term, the stress brought about by the change in their living situation) can be, well, very expressive.

Ellen, for example, remembers how her older cat, Kitty, would throw his arm over her whenever her husband came by. "He was always affectionate," she says, referring to the cat. "But he'd start cuddling and drooling on me whenever Harold, my husband, was around."

"I've had my boyfriend for ten years; we sort of live together," adds Laura, discussing the constant sniping between her man and the big spotted cat Harvey, whom she also loved dearly. "Up until the day he died, Harvey would never let us be together. We'd be in bed and he'd plop himself between us. He'd pee on Chaz's shoes. He wanted me, and nobody else could have me."

"I don't think that I will ever have a relationship with a male figure in my life that will compare to the relationship that I have with my cats," adds Leanne. Recently divorced, she remains on good terms with her ex, who has their old house and thus custody of their two cats, Dallas and Abigail. "The way that you love your cat never, ever fades."

At times, we may be stoking the fires. Consciously or not, we may be fostering jealousy in how we allocate our time and our love. Not that we want our lovers to know this, but sometimes we may very well prefer our cats' purring, nonjudgmental affection to that of even our nearest and dearest human companions. "He loves me, I love him, and he doesn't speak. It's perfect," says Janet, speaking of her cat, Henry, and not her husband, Jeff. "Henry crawls under the covers with me and he'll put his head on my shoulder. We have this connection, and it's undeniable. I swear he's coming between me and my husband. I mean, Jeff loves him, too, but he knows Henry has a special place in my heart."

Sometimes, we are right to prefer the company of our pets. As is true with so many aspects of life, there is much about love we can learn from our cats, from their strong sense of self and their discriminating tastes. For unlike our pets, we are likely to be overly accommodating. We have been socialized to be pleasant, at all costs. To make our dates and mates feel loved and welcomed, even when they do not deserve to be. In the process, we have forgotten how to act as naturally, as gracefully as cats do in their own defense.

"Thank you, I had a lovely time," we say reflexively, no matter that our eyes are crossing with boredom after hours of listening to our blind date's business escapades. "We must do this again," we say ever so politely to the swain who addressed most of his conversation to our cleavage. We allow the kiss at the door, and we hold the smile, our cheeks hurting with the labor until the latch shuts behind us. Or worse, we spend the night, feeling somehow beholden for the effort, and his earnest and probably unfeigned desire. The fact that we are blamed for duplicitous, even catlike behavior when we avoid the follow-up calls and requests for further dates compounds the discomfort of the situation, and the knowledge that our time could better and more enjoyably have been spent paying bills or receiving periodontal work doesn't quite compensate somehow for the guilt these later evasions bring.

I am reminded of a better way. The scene was a party several years ago. I was the hostess and the guests were coming in from the cold by the dozen. We were gathering in the living room, most of us settled in to drink and eat, to talk and to crank the stereo, when suddenly we heard a bellow.

"*Ow!*" I turned to the hallway, where one guest—the new boyfriend of an old friend—stood holding his hand. "Your cat bit me!" He looked at me in aggrieved silence, waiting for me to respond as hostess and woman, with sympathy and horror at my pet's behavior, with offers of poultices or bandages that would both acknowledge and alleviate the insult.

I did not know this man well, but I knew my cat.

"What did you do to him?" I asked, taking the guest's hand. The skin was not broken. Yes, there were several small indentations where Cyrus had clearly pressed his teeth into the hand, but this was a warning bite, nothing more.

"I didn't do anything." The guest seemed shocked at my questioning. "I was petting him, that was all!"

"And where was he?" I asked.

"On the bed, in the pile of coats," he replied. Hiding, I interpreted, in the one quiet room of the apartment. Trying his best to avoid the bustle and big feet of many unaccustomed human guests. Napping in the quiet dark.

"You should have left him alone," I said, and immediately felt the whiplash of guilt. Here was this poor man, perhaps feeling shy around so many new people and therefore seeking the companionship of the one other solitary animal in the house. I was a brute. I brought him a beer and backtracked, making nice and inquiring about the need for antibiotics. My attentions soothed his ego; his hand wasn't really hurt. And the party went on.

The relationship didn't. Within the month this new boyfriend had behaved abominably to my friend, performing one of those classic turns of infidelity and blame that made my friend feel responsible for being betrayed. Listening to her tears and complaints as she began to sort out what had really happened, I realized then that my initial instincts—and Cyrus's—were correct. Someone hadn't been listening when my cat had said no. Someone had been selfish and forced his attentions where they were not wanted. Someone was insensitive and a clod, and then self-pitying to boot. The signs had all been there from the start, but we were too self-deluded, too intent on generosity and pleasing to notice. I wished then that Cyrus had bitten him harder that night. I thought, "Wouldn't it be lovely to be brave enough to draw blood?"

In retrospect, I realized that we can figure out a lot about a potential mate by watching him (or her) with a cat. In talking with other cat-oriented women, I've found that this is a conclusion many of us have reached. "I've been with men who ignore cats and I've learned that's a bad sign," notes Emily. "Anyone who can ignore animals . . . who knows what else they can do."

Her instincts are supported by veterinary ethologist Myrna Milani, who studies animal behavior in the context of relationships. "There's some evidence that the way people relate to cats is the way they relate to all things they perceive as different," says Milani, the author of *CatSmart*. "If you're a career woman and you're in a relationship, ask him what he thinks of your cat.

If he doesn't like it, and you think he'll accept your independence and your career, you're in trouble," she concludes.

Monica didn't start out quite as sure of the connection. A few years ago, while in graduate school, she became engaged to a man who hated cats. She wasn't happy about her fiancé's aversion to her pet of choice, but she couldn't see leaving him for that reason alone. "It always seemed like that wouldn't pass the straight-face test," she explains now. "It didn't seem like a good enough excuse, that I couldn't not marry someone just because he didn't like cats."

In retrospect, she has realized that she had virtually no other frame of reference for how to choose a man. "I went to an all-girls high school, and he was the first guy in college who paid any attention to me," she recalls. In lieu of any real credentials, his gender alone qualified him.

There were signs that perhaps a more worldly woman might have noted. She knew he didn't support her academic aspirations, for example, and was pressuring her to drop out. And his bias against her religion—she was raised a Catholic—was worrisome, too. But it was a little thing that finally clued her in. "I remember going with him to visit my parents, and my mother had fresh strawberries for me in the refrigerator. She knows I adore strawberries." A kind gesture from a loving parent, but her fiancé saw it as a threat. "He told me, 'After we're married, don't expect strawberries.'"

She began to see the light, and was soon "peppered with realizations," as she now says. The ax fell when she was faced with the actual presence of a cat, an all-black female who resembled her childhood pet Benson. This new cat, whom she named Mei Li, appeared on Valentine's Day as a present from her father, who perhaps knew more about his daughter's fiancé than he let on.

"It was a total surprise. I had thought I would spend the rest of my life catless," says Monica. By the time her fiancé objected, she and Mei Li had bonded. Her eyes were opened. Monica wasn't going to give up her new pet for a "self-centered, right-wing jerk," as she finally saw him, and broke the engagement off soon after. "At the time," she says, "I was a bit mad at my dad because I thought he was being manipulative. Now he laughs out loud when I tell him about that, and he admits, 'Yeah I was!' "

Such stories are not entirely unique to our gender. In Colette's classic short novel *The Cat*, a small and dainty feline comes between a husband and wife. In this case, Saha, a Russian blue, was originally the pet of the husband, Alain. It is his young bride, the rather coarse and selfish Camille, who is the interloper. To be honest, the union lacks something from the start. Alain has been swept up by the idea of marriage and perhaps—this being Colette's world—was always more erotically involved with the perfectly groomed, discreet cat. However, only after Camille tries to kill her rival by throwing the poor cat from a window does the marriage fall apart. Alain uncovers the unconscionable act, and leaves immediately, cradling the shaken Saha. Camille's cruelty and selfishness have been revealed. And, besides, Alain really preferred his pet.

This brings up an issue that I feel compelled to clarify: Many men love cats. It would be sexist, and thus clearly untrue to deny that strong bonds do exist between a large number of men and their cats. Just not, I suspect, between as many men and as many cats. However, an awful lot of men love cats, and many more are capable of loving cat-owning women. In fact, some experts, such as Milani, suggest that the number of cat-loving men has begun to grow considerably. Milani cites the shift to the late eighties, when cats gained the ascendancy as the number-one pet in this country, and also when the image of the "new man," the kinder, more evolved male, began to take hold. Perhaps these movements coalesced as men become more comfortable with their feminine, or at least nonconformist sides, and thus also with nonconforming women and our pets.

The most happily mated among us can share some sweet stories: "One of the things I love about Ian is how freely he expresses his affection for the cats," says Jeanne, a San Francisco–based journalist who lives, as well, with Jasper and Joop. "He loves to talk about the cute things they do and he misses them when we're away." Between their extended families and Ian's running, which takes them to marathons all over the world, the two travel frequently. "When we only had Joop and were in Italy for ten days or so, I had to ban him from saying, 'What do you think the kitten is doing?' every day. Now on trips it's 'What do you think the kittens are doing?' " For her part, Jeanne is somewhat calmer about the two felines she calls "my boys."

Talking about her husband, Harold, and their current cat, Wilbur, Ellen starts to laugh as she lists their shared characteristics. "They're really similar in terms of personality," she admits. Wilbur, unlike his predecessor Kitty, is quite mischievous, and although Harold doesn't tip over the garbage or raid the cabinets (much), Ellen notes he is a character in his own way. "Harold is quite nice to Wilbur when I'm not watching, but he does pull his tail and chases him when I'm around," she explains. "It was the same thing when I was a kid with my dad. Dad was bald, and we had a cat who loved to lie on my dad's head and lick my dad's head. If we were around he'd complain and chase him away. If we weren't around, he'd let the cat lick his head. How did we know? We'd catch them!"

As Ellen's memory reveals, more men are probably capable of loving cats than we are aware of, even if they may feel self-conscious about their affections. We have Thomas Stearns Eliot to thank for such playful nomenclature as "jellicles" (for small black-and-white cats) and "gumbie cats" (contemplative tabbies), for example, long before Andrew Lloyd Webber massacred his verse. Even Ernest Hemingway was as distinguished by his love of multitoed felines—his Key West, Florida, home still shelters many a polydactyl puss—as by his incredible machismo.

Perhaps despite Milani's assertions the two traits are even linked: I remember a memorial service for a very cynical, hardboiled friend—he had been a smoker, there had been a fire—where we were all asked to share our memories. People spoke of him as their drinking buddy, as the editor who finally whipped their prose into shape. When my turn came, all I could think of was Rich's cat, an undersized feline-leukemia-positive stray that our editor friend had taken in and given the impossibly aggressive name of Fang. He'd loved that scrawny cat and nursed it into decent health for as long as he could. Fang, in the language of obituary writers, predeceased my friend, but for a while they made quite a pair, the burly drinker and the petite feline. Was there any fear there? Was there some level of overcompensation? Maybe. A good number of the associations between women and cats have been articulated by just such macho men, by the strong male reaction to us, by their attraction to us, perhaps particularly when it is tinged with fear. Perhaps, as Michelle and Jeanne and I have found, the best men, the ones most comfortable with their masculinity, are those willing to face down this fear. Such men do exist (and may perhaps be found in vets' offices or cat shows).

It has also been suggested that the relationship between gay men and cats could make up its own chapter. Some of the parallels are obvious: Gay men have traditionally shared with women the need to camouflage their sexuality and also may feel vulnerable or conflicted about expressing their independence, if not their power. But that is a volume for another—ideally, a gay man—to write. Lesbians, as well, have a legendary relationship with cats. "Where are your cats?" one woman remembers her friends asking, when she and her partner moved in together. Never mind that this woman was and still is allergic, the feline presence was expected. Several lesbian cat owners are among the interviewees in this book, although rarely talking about their sexuality. When we've chatted, we've chatted about our cats more than our mates. And although there's definitely room for a book or three about this female-feline experience, I'm sticking with what I know this time out, which means the connection between women and cats, and the men who love, or fear, us.

What is clear is that we can use our cats as our models for all love relationships. We can see in our pets miniatures of ourselves, and by watching how our mates behave toward them we can spot the potential for abuse. We can also learn from our pets how to conduct ourselves, with dignity, with poise, and with very good boundaries.

Sometimes it is our emotional reaction to our cats, rather than our mates' reactions to the dear creatures, that teaches us the most about our own hearts and about what we really need from love.

Bennie was a Himalayan, a great-looking cat, recalls his woman, Vanessa. Jesse was a gray Persian, and although she wasn't as friendly as her male colleague, together the two of them served to keep Vanessa company during her years of living alone. They came into her life on Christmas, in 1980, not long after her divorce became final. "We kind of grew up together," she says now. "I was extremely attached to them.

"I had nobody else in my life, and my cats were my family," she says, echoing the kind of relationship that many of us have experienced. But because she was divorced and lonely, and because our society doesn't take well to single women, she let herself be fixed up with some man that someone knew. "My friends and parents were enthusiastic about me being resettled," Vanessa remembers. "Everybody was looking for grandchildren."

In all fairness, he wasn't a bad guy. "He was trying to do everything right," she says. But deep in her heart, she knew he wasn't doing it for her. Still, she felt that pressure, and so she agreed to try to live with him, even though the move would come with a heartbreaking catch. He was deeply, wildly allergic to her cats, and therefore when they went looking for a place to call their own, it had to be a new apartment, one without Bennie and Jessie.

"For me it was really nuts to contemplate that." Vanessa laughs, her big grin splitting wide open now that the trauma is years past. "But I didn't know any other way to demonstrate that I was serious. So my mother made it her mission to find a new home for my two cats. She was hellbent on making this work."

Perhaps, the wiry political consultant realizes now, she could have read her own signals better. "I had all these requirements for the new home: There couldn't be any children. It had to be a quiet household. They had to take both of them." She really didn't want to let them go. When her mother found a suitable couple ready to take in the two luxuriant longhairs, Vanessa was not, she says with characteristic understatement, overjoyed.

The new home was ideal: Two childless classical musicians who recently had lost their own cat were looking forward to adopting both of Vanessa's. They had a large house; they lived in the suburbs. They invited Vanessa to dinner when she brought the cats, their toys and dishes and litter boxes.

But she cried all the way home, and the next day she came down with a horrible flu. For three weeks, she ran a fever and could barely get out of bed. "All my defenses were down," she now believes. Giving her pets away, she says "was one of the biggest mistakes of my life. But on the other hand it absolutely saved me from a bigger mistake."

When the fever finally waned, she was ready to face what every pore of her being had been trying to tell her.

"I called the guy and said, 'You know, this is just not going to work out. If this were right, I just wouldn't be in so much pain over these cats. I'm clearly more attached to these cats than I am to you. I should be much more enthusiastic about this.'" The wedding plans were off; Vanessa could be counted in what the American Animal Hospital Association estimates is the 11 percent of cat owners who have ended a relationship because of their cats. But was it the loss of Bennie and Jessie that caused the rift, or was it simply that their absence highlighted her true feelings?

After all that everyone had gone through, Vanessa decided to leave Bennie and Jesse in their new home. One month gone, she reasoned that the cats had more or less readjusted, and their new owners clearly loved them. However, she treated herself to two Maine coon kittens soon after. And that spring, she met Bob, who was the perfect mate for her heart and also for her pets.

Our affection for our pets can help us decipher our more positive feelings toward potential mates, too. "I remember being on a first or second date and being somewhat ambivalent whether it was going to develop into anything or not," Lynne, the adopted mom of the black-and-white Morticio, tells me. "He then mentioned he had just gotten a cat from the animal shelter. He had named her Indigo and told me some cute things she would do.

"Well, that tipped the scales and we became involved in a relationship that lasted for about a year. Although we broke up after that, he and I have remained friends. He's back in Canada now, and he's since added another kitty to the mix. I always ask how 'the girls' are doing and he always asks after my cat, asking after 'the boy.' "

When the relationship does work out, then our feelings about our pets can help us delve even deeper. I clearly remember that the day Jon cleaned the litter box, I nearly went into shock. That was about seven years ago, and I should clarify that Jon, who was then my boyfriend of about a year, had not done anything that I didn't do, well, almost weekly. And Cyrus's crapper certainly had begun to smell. But when I came home from the corner grocery, bags of ice and supplies in hand to prep for a dinner with friends, I never expected to see him walking out the door with a garbage bag full of cat poop in his.

"It smelled," he said.

"I know," I replied. "I figured I'd change it when I got back."

Honestly, I probably wouldn't have had time before our dinner party started. Instead, I would have tried to ignore it, hoping that our guests would too. Or maybe I secretly knew this man was on to my olfactory fatigue and hoped, subconsciously, that he'd do something about it. I had a great capacity for writing off as "homey" such things as piles of newspapers, lint-covered furniture and, yes, the pungent scent of a ripe litter box.

And so he had changed it. I had to wonder, could this man be the love of my life? And, if so, how exactly did I feel about letting someone get that far into my personal space?

As generous and unexpected as it was, Jon's voluntary litter-box cleaning brought up the uncomfortable question about where our relationship ended and where my own private life began. We'd been together long enough that I didn't doubt his willingness to get serious, my usual concern after one decade too many of commitment-phobic men. With this pressure gone, however, I was left with the task of determining the level of the relationship.

I'd spent weeks, off and on, wondering how serious it could get, how serious I wanted it to get, in every possible manifestation. I was facing my own fear of intimacy, even if I didn't want to call it that, and wondered what was a phobia on my part, and what was just a healthy need for clear personal boundaries.

And that's how I found myself pondering the rules of cat ownership. When, after all, does one person's pet become the couple's? Was my cat our cat? And how did I feel about sharing the small gray love of my life?

Don't get me wrong. I had no unhealthy attachment to cleaning up feline waste products: the litter, the fur balls, the unexplained vomiting that wakes you at dawn with its bouncing, hacking sound. But Cyrus and I had lived together for a long time by then, nearly nine years before Jon came into our lives. I wasn't sure I was willing to let some man in on that.

There were also Cyrus's emotions to consider. A cat, after all, is not a possession to be shared without consultation. A cat is a fellow creature, a beast of as many moods and personalities as any of us. Cyrus and I, for example, had taken several years to come to an understanding about lap sitting. It had taken me quite a while to accept that although he would happily sit by me on the couch, I could not expect him to jump in my lap like some mindless kitten. Once I learned to let him purr contentedly by my side he graciously forgave me my previous uncouth attempts to haul him onto me and pin him there.

Now, just because I was pairing off with a man, I had no right to assume that Cyrus would comply. As his forthright opinion in the matter of lap sitting had demonstrated, he wasn't the type of creature that would simply allow himself to be passed back and forth between lovers like a sweatshirt or favorite CD. Cyrus had a voice in the sharing, while my clothing and the band X did not. And Cyrus's voice could be exceedingly imperious.

There had been, for example, the gentleman on whose clothes he had defecated (an ultimately appropriate judgment call) and many more from whom he had simply withheld affection. Which made for comforting memories: perhaps I wouldn't have to make waves with Jon about his de facto adoption of my cat. Cyrus would make himself heard if he didn't like the way things were going. I wouldn't have to say a thing. So I was caught off guard when I realized that Cyrus was not only already aware of what was going on, but he actually seemed to like it. As he flipped over, offering Jon his belly to rub, I realized he was open-ing up to my boyfriend, trusting him to a degree that I still found difficult. In fact, the little fellow seemed perfectly content, round green eyes staring upside down at me as if to ask, "Well, did you want to cart that shit out?" Obviously, the issues were mine, of sharing my small gray friend. And Jon's, of taking on a responsi-bility, sharing a role. A foster cat.

But Jon really didn't seem to have any problems with feline stepfathering. I recalled that an ex-girlfriend of his had owned three cats. He'd moved in with her, and one of the cats had taken it badly. There was hissing, soiling of personal property, scratch-ing at the eyes. Taking matters into his own hands, Jon finally cornered the offending feline and sprayed him with a water pis-tol until said cat howled for mercy. Household dominance estab-lished, the once spiteful kitty revered Jon, following him around to sit at his feet and gaze adoringly at his shins. After Jon and the lady split up, he heard that that cat had missed him most, howl-ing and crying as though he had lost one of his own pride.

Jon had no issues with cat ownership. In fact, he probably saw my cat as one of my more attractive features. I knew Cyrus would like that, if he ever figured it out. I wasn't sure how I felt. Meanwhile, I was left wallowing in my insecurities and feeling a bit put out over Jon's cavalier assumption of litter duty. I always thought I'd wanted a man who was unafraid of responsibility, of sharing, and of the dirtier jobs in life. But what if—while I was preoccupied unraveling my fear of intimacy from the rest of the emotional morass—Jon assumed more pet duties? What if he took over the vet visits and the grooming? How would I feel the first time the cat curled up to sleep like a small heated beanbag on *his* belly?

Later that night, as we stared blankly at the TV screen in what was becoming a comfortable if indolent habit, Cyrus jumped on the couch. On Jon's side. I was crushed and sank farther into the sofa, jealousy flooding my heart, along with a cold sadness: I'd been replaced. I said nothing, but in a long-term relationship both partners can sense emotional storms brewing. As if to quell the impending squall, Cyrus got up and slowly walked over my boyfriend to settle in beside me. I stroked his smooth gray head, happy again.

But Cyrus didn't resume his usual nap position. Instead, he sat up. Carefully, deliberately, he began kneading my side. Hard. He crouched on his hindquarters like a gopher, his big ears tilted back, and he seemed to be concentrating as he sank one paw and then the other into the soft flesh of my waist. His determined paws sunk deep into my side, but I made no effort to stop him. Sure it hurt, but I wanted him to like me best.

6

MEOWS AND WHISPERS

"This isn't going to work," I told Jon. "He's angry with me." This was only a few nights ago, just past dawn, when the gray light filtering into the kitchen and the adjoining mud room barely illuminated myself, Jon, and Cyrus, who sat behind his litter box, on the mat of newspaper, glaring at me.

"How can you tell?" asked Jon sleepily. We'd been awake for a good twenty minutes now, since I'd risen at Cyrus's agitated prowlings and carried him into the small foyer adjoining our back porch. Jon had followed soon after, and was now leaning on the doorframe, bleary eyed, watching as I lifted our cat into the litter box and watching as Cyrus stepped out of it, back and forth a half dozen times or more. At sixteen, Cyrus had developed litter-box problems—inappropriate elimination, as our vet called it—and I was hoping to retrain him. I was hoping, to be honest, that the problem was emotional rather than physical, that his new habit of shitting on the living room rug sprang from anger or anxiety at the frequent, if brief trips Jon and I had been taking all summer, and not by one of the chronic afflictions of age. If I can get him to shit in the box, I told myself, then he doesn't have an intestinal lymphoma. If I can retrain him, then he doesn't have irritable bowel syndrome, or mega colon, or whatever else can go wrong in the body of a small gray cat. At 5:00 in the morning, or 4:30, or whenever it was when our routine had started, the rational mind is not functioning at its finest.

At least mine wasn't. Cyrus, on the other hand, seemed wide awake, his green eyes glaring at me, gaze sharp as a tack. After the last go-round, he'd given up trying to walk back into the kitchen, to eat or take up his customary nighttime roost under my arm or at the foot of our bed. Now he just sat beside his litter box, on the spread-out newspaper we'd laid down to catch the litter kicked over the side. He glared and, as much as space allowed, lashed his tail, the gray plume flicking into wall, into the side of the box, and back again.

"We're not getting anywhere." I stepped back into the kitchen, for once not feigning my retreat as a ploy to lure Cyrus from his corner. "He's furious." I led my somnolent husband back to bed and, soon after, felt the quiet thud of Cyrus landing next to me. All was forgiven, I figured, as he kneaded my upper arm, tucked himself in beside me, and proceeded to purr us both back to sleep.

Communication is vital between us and our cats, as it is in any relationship. Being women we are likely to be fairly well attuned to just how important it is. We are, after all, the primary market for every pop psychology book aimed at improving mutual understanding; we are the ones who focus on nuance, on tone of voice, on the nonverbal signals that help us relate to each other. Even ignoring such best-sellers as Deborah Tannen's *You Just Don't Understand* or the John Gray *Men Are from Mars* cottage industry, most of us sense instinctively how vital an open flow of feelings and ideas is. We live, perhaps even more than the men we know and love, in the framework of relationships; we define ourselves in terms of those around us. As Carol Gilligan notes in her classic *In a Different Voice*, as girls we tend to develop our sense of right and wrong, of who we are, within the context of our communities; whereas boys have a more discrete, if not detached development. We want to connect; we want to understand. And, because we do, and because we do not yet run the world, we tend to be more sensitive to the flip side, to understand the pain of being ignored or not understood.

For all of these reasons, we appreciate a good interaction, and we are, on the whole, committed to communicating well with our cats. On the most practical level, we recognize that an open exchange helps to ease the tensions that come about whenever living beings cohabit. With our cats, as with our mates or room-mates or children, we need it to set down our boundaries, to establish the rules that, in this case, keep the shit in the box. Being the women we are, we generally expect not only obedience, but comprehension. We seek out this kind of communication as a way of strengthening our relationships, of building on our feelings of trust, acceptance, and love. Speaking of her cat Twig, for example, Barb describes a quite straightforward interaction, with a level of trust that many of us may envy.

"We understood each other the first time he knocked over the garbage," she says. "I went into the kitchen and he was in the garbage trying to get some chicken and so I told him to get out of there. And he did, looking quite shocked. I told him that chicken bones are bad for kitties. He hasn't gotten in there since."

For most of us, as happened for me on that recent night, communicating with our cats involves a more indirect combination of body language, observation, and consistency in training. We impress upon them what we like and what we won't permit. They, ideally, absorb what we expect of them. We learn to read the signals—the lashing tail, the glaring eyes—that express their side of the argument as they learn what the handclap and the peremptory "no!" signify, and together we set the parameters of the relationship.

It's on such common sense that the work of animal behaviorists, aka cat shrinks, base their work. These professionals are usually called in to consult in problem situations, and often they act as translators as much as trainers. As revealed in stories recollected in books by behaviorists like Larry Lachman, Pam Johnson-Bennett, or Nicholas Dodman, director of the animal behavior clinic at the Tufts University School of Veterinary Medicine, the emphasis is often more on understanding why a cat is acting a certain way and how to make your needs clear in return rather than just punishments or rewards. Is a cat really angry at you when he hisses and lashes out, or is he clawing because he's afraid? Does your cat know you are upset when you smack his kicking feet away, or is he mistaking your response for play?

Clarifying what we are trying to say and deciphering their responses are the basis for communication. "Understanding is very important," says Dr. Amy Marder, vice president of animal behavior for the Massachusetts Society for the Prevention of Cruelty to Animals and clinical professor at Tufts University School of Veterinary Medicine. She stresses that in her line of work, clients want behaviors—usually common problems like urinating on furniture or biting—to change. Often, the solution comes with comprehension: "A person who doesn't clean the litterbox enough doesn't understand that cats like clean litterboxes." She also tells me, as we chat, that she thinks that many of us (and clearly she means me and the 95 percent of her clientele who are women) tend to anthropomorphize our pets. This misreading, she stresses, can open up a whole new set of problems. "We misinterpret our own behaviors, so how can we interpret other species?" she asks.

Not all of our connection can be explained in terms of rules and treats, however. In fact, nearly every cat lover reports some bond that can't be entirely dismissed by the sounds of food being prepared. Rosie, for example, is "a shy, skinny little creature who is usually more comfortable on her own, under a chair," her person Silvana reports. "But sometimes I'll be lying in bed early in the morning, just before getting up, or else sitting on the couch in the evening, and I think to myself, 'Where's Rosie?' Within a minute or two, she scampers over to me. It may sound crazy, but I'm convinced that Rosie can 'hear' me call her intuitively," she says.

Even the most scientific of animal experts agree that an element of intuition comes into play when people and animals interact. "One of the things you'll find with veterinarians," says Dr. Jean Duddy, a veterinarian at Boston's Angell Memorial Animal Hospital, "is that they communicate better with one species." Duddy, a hearty farm-girl type who lives with eight cats and one dog, runs the radioactive iodine therapy treatment program at Angell, which means she sees her share of stressed-out hyperthyroid kitties. "I can pretty much tell you when a cat is in my exam room what his next move is going to be," she says, and I've seen her heft many a frightened tabby, so I believe her.

"I get fooled by dogs on occasion. There are many vets in the hospital who are the exact opposite. They suddenly find a cat attached to them."

If only we could understand what our cats are trying to say to us, it would not only save our furniture some wear and tear, it could save our lives. Marie still recalls how her two cats, Sebastian and Romulus, knew when her house's wiring had shorted out. Whether the two cats—the orange tabby and his "domino" masked partner—smelled the first whiffs of smoke, or whether some other sense alerted them, she doesn't know.

"There was something in their tone, the way they were both crying that morning." Marie's an Internet professional, with a grounded business sense that doesn't allow for much sentimental nonsense, but that morning, she knew something was going on that her sharp ears and funky glasses couldn't take in. "They were both crying and desperate to go out." Neither Marie nor her husband could make sense of the feline hints, but finally capitulated, freeing the cats into the yard even before their usual morning treats. Sheer luck got Marie and Ivan out of the house and toward their respective offices as well before the blaze broke through the walls, burning fierce and fast.

Marie and Sebastian, who she calls her "soul cat," had always had a special connection, albeit one that fit her no-nonsense nature. "When I first adopted Sebastian, we had a discussion about the rules of the relationship," she says. "He was to live with me for fifteen years, was never to run away permanently, and he was to let me know ahead of time before he died so I could be prepared.

"When Sebastian passed away one month into his fifteenth year, he had never run away, had led a healthy life, and he was most definitely getting old," she continues. "He did let me know he was ready to depart this earth, but not before surveying his domain one last time from the rooftop. He passed on the next morning."

Such negotiations, I'm learning, are not uncommon. Most of us accept that our cats understand—and accept—more than they are willing to let on.

"We have a deal," explains Erna, running her large and well-worn hand through the luxurious calico coat of Mumma Cat. Long-haired and glossy, it is hard to believe that five years ago Mumma and her equally huge offspring, Babie, were once part of a feral colony living in the former farmland behind Erna's house, land she now digs and plants for herself. "We came to an understanding," Erna says, recalling the frigid early spring day when she found the scrawny, bedraggled mother cat hiding her new litter of kittens under the low glass panes of a seedling shelter. She had seen the weather-beaten cat hanging around her yard before, and she recognized a call for help. Erna, a take-charge type, began removing the kittens to her own sheltered porch. "I told her, I wasn't going to lock her in the house, just the kittens." Mumma, as the mother cat was dubbed, followed.

Soon, the big black bruiser who seemed to be her mate started nosing around. Erna had a frank talk with him as well. "I told him, you can come into the house. But you have to be fixed and you have to be social, and you have to visit a vet. And you cannot lay a finger on the other kitties. At some point he decided to accept my terms, and he made it really clear. Once he flipped, he flipped," she recalls. "He became my love slave."

Mr. Kittie, as the former tom came to be known, died from feline immunodeficiency virus ("feline AIDS") last winter, but his final years were comfortably domestic. Even Mumma grew well socialized in time, and hardly goes outdoors anymore. "Now she's quite the house cat," says Erna, stroking the long silky fur. "But I think her image of herself as a semiwild kitty is important to her." Looking at the plump picture of contentment now tucked into herself on the sofa arm, it's hard for me to see. But then, she didn't call to me.

Building on that intuitive connection may be an art. It's also become a profession, one that by some estimates several hundred people are now practicing across the United States. For such interspecies facilitators, who usually prefer the title "animal communicator" to "cat psychic," the means is telepathy. Mental images, rather than bristling fur, are their clues to an animal's emotions and thoughts. And often, professionals say, to deeper peace and communion with nature for the pets' owners as well.

"People start out just wanting to learn what their cat is saying, but they end up becoming more whole," explains Penelope Smith, a professional animal communicator. "It's a transformational journey, a spiritual path." Smith, who lives with three cats, considers herself one of the more "open" humans, able to hear animals and help them work through their spiritual and emotional woes as well as capable of leading fellow humans into the same realm of understanding. "I work with people to help them realize who they are. The animals are perfect teachers, because they know who they are.

"Once you lose your prejudices, we're all fellow beings," she says. "We just have different outfits."

Since the mid-seventies, Smith has made a career out of her ability to relate to animals, making her the doyenne of animal psychics. The author of *Animal Talk* and *When Animals Speak*, she also runs workshops that train others to communicate telepathically with animals. "All people can get it," she believes. "For some, it's more easy. Some people are just more open to the intuitive."

Sharon Callahan discovered her ability to understand animals early on in life. The author of a book on homeopathic treatments, *Flower Essence Therapy for Animals*, Callahan says she has been able to tune into animals "since I was a kid." For her, communications come in a warming, nearly electric flow from an animal, which sometimes carries visual images or emotions and sometimes entire trains of thought. Occasionally, particularly with ill or dying pets, the flow seems to come through an intermediary, "an angel or whatever you want to call it," although the flow remains very fast and spontaneous. Illness and death, or near-death, seems to have been a catalyst in her work, Callahan acknowledges. Although she's made animal communication her profession for the last twenty years, she credits a nearly fatal illness fourteen years ago with giving a new depth and profundity to her work. "Prior to that experience," says the Northern California psychic, "I did the usual thing: helping people with animal behavioral problems, cats that weren't using the litter box, that sort of thing. Now I do more of a reading of the entire experience, including the people. What I learned from that experience is that animals are in people's lives to show them something spiritual, to guide them."

With her current cat companion, the sixteen-year-old Lily, Callahan explains, she is learning more about "the divine feminine," or the essential female nature of the universe. Men as well as women, she says, can benefit by opening themselves to this side of life, which ranges from maternal warmth to the destructive face of a goddess like Durga. When I tell her that I see a link between our strong feelings about cats and our primordial goddess worship, she agrees and expresses the hope that humans are evolving back to recognition of this power. "Cats to me really hold the energy of the divine feminine in all its aspects," she says. "That's the only thing that's going to save us," she says. We seem, for the length of a phone call, to be of one mind.

Such psychic connections may have practical applications. Sue, originally from Yorkshire, England, credits a chance meeting with a psychic for the safe return of her darling Bluebell. The gray tabby with the huge yellow eyes had disappeared one night, cat-napped by an ex-boyfriend. He knew exactly how to hurt Sue most. "He said the cat was at a friend's house, and the friend was on holiday," said the emergency room nurse. "He said I'd get him back in two weeks, but I knew he was lying."

Sue did what we all would do: She went out nights calling Bluebell's name. She spent "a fortune" on posters and ads. She feared that her ex had grabbed the petite tabby and dumped him somewhere on the outskirts of town. Bluebell had been a house-cat, and Sue worried about how he'd cope outdoors, whether in the woods or the city. As the weeks turned to months and summer turned to fall she became resigned. "I was just hoping he was found and was in a good home," she said.

Then, one night, another nurse told her that the hospital had admitted a psychic. "I introduced myself and said, 'Oh I've lost my cat.' And she said, 'Come back in about twenty minutes. Let me think about it.' I felt a bit terrible because the poor thing had just come in to hospital and here I am hounding her. But I did go back and she said, 'Oh he's got such big eyes, hasn't he?'"

The psychic proceeded to tell Sue that soon she'd have a window of opportunity to get Bluebell back, but even if she didn't act on it, the tiny tabby would be okay. Forcing herself to be comforted by that news, Sue went back to work.

A few weeks passed. "Then a strange thing happened," she

recalls. "I got these calls, three days apart. One saying that they thought they'd seen my cat, but it turned out it wasn't Bluebell. Then another said there was a dead cat that sounded like my cat. I drove down, and it looked very much like my cat, but it wasn't my cat. The following week, one of the girls who I work with called me. She had read an ad saying 'lost cats.' And I called, and described him, and it was him." That week, she decided, had been her "window of opportunity." The ad had been placed by a woman who took in abandoned, lost, and feral cats. She had found Bluebell confused and starving by a roadside and had taken him in three months earlier to nurse him back to glossy health.

Thanks to the kindly caretaker, whose earlier postings had gone unnoticed by the hospital staff, Sue and Bluebell were reunited. The next day, the psychic called, "Just to see how I was," Sue recalls, with a trace of wonder.

My own experience with an animal communicator was, well, more challenging than such classic success stories had led me to believe. I'm willing to take the blame. Perhaps I chose the wrong empath, although the woman I dealt with had trained with Smith and charged more for our forty-five-minute consultation than does my therapist. But I should have known something was off when she suggested an early Saturday morning reading. I do not like early mornings, and, to the best of my knowledge, neither does Cyrus. Yes, he does tend to rise around 5:00 A.M. and try to rouse me to play or at least to provide breakfast. But right around the time that the alarm is usually ringing, he has snuggled in again, making himself into an irresistibly purring comforter addition. I customarily succumb to the point of pure sloth, alternately dozing and listening to him purr (or snore) until long past 10:00 A.M. I did not think either of us would be at our best at an early morning appointment.

I countered by suggesting a weekday or weeknight, only to hear that my communicator worked as an office temp during the day and had rehearsals for a play she was acting in most evenings. Animal communication is more avocation than vocation, I gathered. But once we settled on an early evening, nonrehearsal night, I thought we'd be okay. Her instructions were clear: Call at 6:30, promptly, and I would have my thirty-five-minute session. Thirty-five minutes? Well, of course, I had paid for forty-five, but before I called, the communicator would have spent ten minutes with Cyrus alone, communicating empathically, and without the need for long-distance phone rates.

I got home with minutes to spare that evening and dived into the shower. Clean and clothed once more, I went into the kitchen to feed Cyrus before I remembered that he was to be calm and seated for the ten minutes preceding my consultation; I stopped scooping his special diet can and considered leaving it on the counter. The look he gave me communicated quite clearly that this would not be an acceptable option, and I put the dish down. I don't know how calm he was going to be with only half a can, but I'm the one who would hear about it afterward, one way or another. He gave me no guff, and at the stroke of 6:30, as if on cue he followed me into the living room and jumped onto the sofa beside me.

What psychic messages he had been transmitting during his abbreviated meal, I could only imagine. "He was going 'Yum! Yum! Yum!'" I pictured the psychic telling me. "That's all I could get." But when we were both seated and I made my call, I was in for a completely different surprise.

She started in immediately with the messages she said Cyrus had for me: "He really misses his red ball; he says the dog took it from him." Now, Cyrus has been a housecat all his life, since I adopted him from his litter. As far as I know no dog burglars have been in the house, nor did I remember any roseate toy that had gone missing. "Does he know a big red dog? Perhaps a rooster, or a rooster dog?" I had no idea what a rooster dog is, but I stretched my imagination. "Well, I have red hair. And our landlady upstairs from our last apartment had a sort of golden cocker spaniel. But as far as I know they never had any interaction." We would come back to the red dog later, I was told. Cyrus seemed to think it was important, she said. The cat seated beside me was letting his eyes close. Concentrating, I assumed. "Cyrus also says he really misses the playground. He misses watching the children play in the playground." Could he mean the yard we shared with our neighbors? I couldn't think of any other explanation. "No," she replied. "There are jungle gyms and all sorts of things to climb on, and he misses watching the children climb and play."

Now onto my questions. Some of these were, of course, age related. Did Cyrus as he was entering his late teens have any requests for different treatment, for a change in diet, or in my behavior that would make his life more pleasant? "He needs more exercise," said the communicator, speaking for the cat who was by now tucked up meatloaf style and snoozing by my side. "He'd really like a playmate so he could run and chase things." Cyrus didn't wake to contradict her, and I let it slide.

"Are you sure you're channeling my cat?" I asked. I started imagining other kittens in the neighborhood, wondering if we'd crossed wires. "I asked Cyrus to tell me something that would let his mommy know I was talking to him," she countered. "Something that only you would know about." And what did he say? "Martin," she responded without hesitation. "Martin, the big man, outside."

This gave me pause, for I had known a Martin. In college. He was a good dancer and had dated a friend of mine. We had been housemates one summer with about four other classmates in a shambling sublet up in Porter Square; I'd been working at a university press and he was filling up on premed requirements. Cyrus was not then even a gleam in some longhaired tom's eye. I looked out the window. Martin wasn't outside. Come to think of it, he wasn't that big either, unless you count tall and lanky. He probably weighed less than I do now. "Martin?" I asked, confused. I had run into Martin a few years ago and we'd had coffee. He was a doctor now, married. I looked to see if anyone was hiding in the shrubbery. "Could Martin be one of the neighborhood cats?" I asked. "No, Martin's a big man. Cyrus said you would know." Sometimes I think Cyrus has a very active imagination.

The session continued, punctuated by breaks in which the communicator consulted the sleeping cat by my side. As instructed, I was careful not to distract him though I couldn't resist the occasional pet. At one point he woke, annoyed by my attentions, and jumped off the sofa. I was tempted to tell the communicator that he had left the room, but I feared distracting her. If a psychic bond could carry over a long-distance phone line, it would carry into the kitchen. He came back soon, anyway, and by then we were onto other issues. Did Cyrus have any aches and pains he needed me to know about? I hadn't wanted to trap her, but I figured she didn't really need to be informed about our latest vet visit, the one that gave me the update on his shrinking kidneys and his possible intestinal problems.

"Sometimes I take into my own body what your cat is feeling," said the woman, adding, "his neck is stiff, as are his upper back and shoulders." Of course, if Cyrus had spent the day at a computer, as my psychic had, this would likely be true. Still it seemed easy enough to promise extra pets and strokes that evening. "Plus," she continued, "he's afraid of the green chair. It's so high that he's worried about losing his balance." By this point, our little communicant had flipped his head over, bat-style, chin up with one fang exposed. One closed eye opened a slit to stare at me, upside down. "We don't have a green chair." "Did you ever?" I wasn't going to argue with that green-gold eye. "Maybe I did," I replied, the eye slowly closed again.

Was there anything else I should know? "Don't give me the vitamins!" she said firmly. Sorry, kitty, you're sixteen. When you need medication, you're getting it. "But I can understand that he doesn't like it," I assured the communicator. Who would like having an eyedropper forced into his or her mouth? On to pleas-anter topics, I thought. Were there any particular treats or tastes Cyrus would want me to know about?

"Oh yes, he likes when you sing to him," she told me. "He likes when you dance and twirl around." A hit, I'll confess, if you can define my tuneless crooning of what is known in our house as "the kitty song" (complete lyrics: "kitty, kitty, kitty") as singing. However, since she was talking to a woman willing to plunk down seventy dollars on a phone conversation about her cat with a total stranger, odds were good she was talking to a woman who would sing to said feline as well.

"He likes the sweet music," she continued. "Does he seem to like sweet music?" As a sometime music critic, I'd be the first to acknowledge the subjectivity of that classification, but this is a cat who has been know to stare at the speakers transfixed when Ornette Coleman is playing. Perhaps he hears the atonal skronk and squeal of avant-garde jazz as a particularly beguiling form of music. Perhaps he hears in it the panicked screams of trapped prey. I can't imagine describing it as sweet. "Yes," I replied. "He does seem to respond to music." Time was running out, and I had a final big question.

Pursuant to my project, I explained to the communicator, I

really wanted to know if Cyrus had any thoughts on the connection between women and cats. This one was a no-brainer; after only about thirty seconds of silence, the communicator came back with a long, very flattering answer. "Women are softer," she began. "And they let you play on the shag rug. Do you have a little shag rug?" she continued. What women doesn't, I thought to myself as my communicator rambled on with a string of vague compliments all praising the womanly qualities my cat most admired. But as she and I said our thanks and farewells, I felt a wild thought pop into my mind. I suddenly knew what had been happening. Cyrus resented the intrusion into his evening routine, if not his brain. That furry scalawag was having us both on, feeding us misinformation and dirty jokes. Martin, indeed. Cyrus could communicate for himself, thank you very much, I thought.

I must confess I dismissed the words of the psychic, and after apologizing to my cat we resumed our normal interaction. Then, on a chance, I drove by our old apartment, the one we'd lived in for almost two years before buying our current home. I was going on errands, heading for the grocery store, when I noticed, perhaps for the first time, the slide and jungle gym, the climbing toys and the sandbox in the park, across the street from the first-floor apartment we had rented. In full view of the wide front window where Cyrus used to sit for hours. I'm wondering, now, about that red ball.

All of which makes me hesitant to say that communicators can't channel, or that some cats aren't open to delicate mind probing. Sure, horror stories abound: one vet tells me with disgust about another client, whose cat she was treating for renal failure. The client's denial of the medical situation was aided and abetted by a pricey communicator. "She kept telling this poor woman that all her cat needed was some rest," the vet complains to me. "That cat was dying. It was clearly in pain, but that woman kept shelling out the bucks to hear otherwise."

No matter who is trying to communicate, the moral in this could be that we really only hear what we want to. And for every story like the vet's or like mine, there is probably one like Sue's. Animal communicators wouldn't be proliferating at the rate they are if some people did not find guidance or comfort from their words. Are they speaking for our animals? At some level, it doesn't matter. Because, to some extent, such communication has always been more about us than about our pets, more about what we need than about what they are trying to tell us. Ultimately, we tend to use our cats as humans have always used pets: as therapists. That is, in our relationship they become the mirror or receptacle onto which we can pour our thoughts and emotions in order to understand them ourselves. We talk to our cats so that we may listen to ourselves. And one of the great beauties of cats is that they do appear to listen. It is in their nature to sit calmly and seem interested as we talk, and we love them so much in part because they do pay attention to what we say when often nobody else will.

"When I was living alone, I was constantly talking to the cat, singing made-up songs and learning to be silly, which you certainly wouldn't do with anyone you didn't know very, very well," says Juli, whose beloved black-and-white Sophie followed her from Boston to New York and finally into married life in Tennessee. For Juli, Sophie was a first conduit of self-expression, the spiritual guide who helped her discover her own creativity.

"A lot of what Sophie taught me," she explains, "was to be freeform. To ad lib." Although she's been in the music industry all her adult life, Juli's always been on the business side. She's known for her strength at negotiations, not any sense of melody, but now she talks to me of making up rhymes for her cat or allowing her untrained voice to range full throttle because Sophie's big black ears always seemed so attentive. As she talks, her New York cadences still slightly apparent, I find myself humming the kitty song. I refrain from singing it to Juli (Cyrus, sitting by me, might not appreciate it), but when I begin to explain, she immediately understands.

"Having a cat to talk to allows you to be inane," she explains. "For a long time she was the only thing that was a constant in my life. I moved here; I moved there. I didn't have a bed to sleep in. I didn't have furniture, but I always had Sophie. She was my rock. I lived essentially alone as a single person for so long, and I know that when I don't have animals around I don't talk to myself. Everything gets internalized, so if I don't go out, I don't say a word. But if the cat was around I'd be like, 'So, Soph, what do you think?' "

That's the question, and whether the answer comes from our own needs or from the most basic animal nature of our pets is almost superfluous. What matters is that through communicating with cats, we may become better listeners. We may come to recognize their needs and desires. We may come to better understand ourselves.

·😺·

Even as I try to reason this out, Cyrus is trying to tell me something. I think he is waiting for me to finish. Or perhaps he is trying to tell me he likes the taste of paper.

Like all cats, Cyrus has a complex relationship with paper, one that began early as he learned to feint and trap folding pages of newspaper, slamming each one to earth with his fierce leap, and commanding the attention that I had previously given to the weak and fickle page. It is a relationship that has grown increasingly complex throughout our time together, as his kittenish antics have given way to annoyed scratching (at the tantalizing backs of shelved books), eating (he's crazy about glue-saturated envelope flaps), and now, the demanding paw that slaps down the usurping page and flattens the journal onto the lap which by rights is his. He bites the corner of a page and looks me in the eye.

The problem is in part an adversarial one. I am a writer and, perhaps worse, an avid reader. Paper occupies my time and often my lap. And this will not be tolerated. For what many cat critics refuse to acknowledge is that our cats want us to notice them. They do not, unlike dogs, want to be mauled. They want to be respected and acknowledged. They want access. As animal behaviorists often point out, they want to play—to simulate the active life they would have had out on the veldt, chasing prey—and they want us to hunt with them. The issues, as are so often the case in human relationships, are time and attention. We want them to listen to us; they need us to listen to them as well. Why, then, our cats seem to ask of us, as we have so often asked about our human mates, is it so difficult to make ourselves understood?

The luckier cats, and I do count Cyrus among them, have not always been aware of this problem. Many days I have opened my front door to find him trotting down the hallway, chirping away as I punch the alarm code in and put down my bags. "Where have you been? Wait till you hear what has been happening in my day," I believe he is telling me with his nonstop chirruping, his squeaks and eeks that accompany his stiff-legged gait to the living room. There he will promptly flop and wait for his belly rub, his back arched to expose his fluffy white underfur like some ecstatic squirrel. This is our routine and sometimes, especially when I have been away all day, his atonal monologue, jumping all over his own feline twelve-tone scale, will continue as I rub his white belly, his outstretched paws kneading the air in satisfaction. He does not notice if I am listening or not; he assumes he has my full attention and understanding.

However, recently I think he has begun to grasp my lack of comprehension. "Eh," he says, looking closely in my face. "Eh!" he repeats, in frustration. And I do know then what he is asking: What part of meow don't you understand?

7

OBSESSION

Some cats eat Iams. Others get generic cans. I know a woman, a vegetarian, who occasionally cooks chicken for her cat, Missy, although she won't taste it herself. But I've heard of only one cat who, for a while, dined regularly on sirloin.

"My husband would find bits of leftover steak on the lawn," Janet is telling me. "And he'd ask, 'Where did this steak come from?'" She'd feign ignorance, although the truth was that she'd put out the beef strips in her efforts to tame the skittish stray she'd dubbed Henry. Later, when the weather turned frosty, the native New Englander would leave her grandmother's fur coat out on the porch as well, to make sure the orange-striped tiger didn't get too cold. He was tamed eventually—who wouldn't be?—and joined the elfin brunette, her husband, Jeff, and their other cat, Stanley, in the warmth of their cozy home, taking up his rightful place most nights in the middle of the bed. "No, I don't spoil my cats," Janet tells me. She plays guitar in a hard-rock band and, despite her sense of humor, has an image of toughness that belies her size. I wouldn't dream of contradicting her.

Whether we're dealing with fur or simply Fancy Feast, the question of how far we will go for our cats is one most of us have to face at some point. I learned that my limits were not where I had thought I had set them late one night in a frigid New England February when I tried to pull a fast one on my kitty. The situation, I confess, was of my own making. Somewhere between work and play I had neglected that most important of errands, the purchase of cat food. Specifically, those 3.7 ounce brand-name cans of tuna and cheese bits. (My cat, like most I suspect, has had a lifelong tendency toward single-minded fanaticism. One flavor and one only will do, at least until it no longer does. Then I, usually with a larder well stocked with the now-unacceptable old flavor, have to bring home a half-dozen new flavors before a replacement favorite is chosen. Only then does life settle down again for a few months.)

At any rate, I knew this was the flavor, the only acceptable flavor, and yet somehow I had let the larder empty without refilling it. A sin I did not realize I had committed until approximately 2:30 one Saturday night (make that Sunday morning), when I stumbled in, pulled off my boots, and tried to decide if I had the energy left to brush my teeth.

"*Mrrup!*" One of the great joys of owning a cat is that there is always someone waiting up to meet you. The greeting is usually one of joy, no reprimands about the hour or the state of your makeup, hair, or breath. But this time there was a distinctly demanding note in the welcome. "*Mrrupp?!*"

"Give me a minute, Cyrus," I told him, as I reached under the couch for the plush slippers that my tired, cold feet demanded. "One second, sweetie," as I peeled off my smoky sweater and jeans and reached for the ripped, soft flannel nightie that signified comfort to me. *"Mrrup?"*

I padded to the kitchenette, barely large enough for the two of us to stand there, and I felt his sleek body start its graceful figure eights around my now-bare ankles. I opened the cabinet and suddenly started to wake up. There were no cans. I pushed the packages of ramen noodles aside. No tuna and cheese bits. I looked behind the soy sauce, behind the tomato sauce and the can of pineapple chunks that had gotten stuck to the shelf long before. The familiar pink-and-white label was not to be seen. There were no cans for Cyrus. A quick perusal of my junior-sized fridge yielded nothing either, no half-eaten servings saved from a warmer day. No misplaced tins behind the skim milk and beer.

I was too tired to think. Cyrus wrapped himself around my ankle again, his mewing picking up in intensity. *Tuna and cheese, tuna and cheese.* I leaned into the light of the small, frosted refrigerator and inspiration struck. I saw cellophane. I remembered a small can, the wrong size and color, behind the spaghetti sauce, and I got to work.

"It's tuna and cheese! Tuna and cheese! Your favorite!" I knew my tone was overdoing it. I suspected that even as I shredded the Kraft cheddar slices into the water-packed white Albacore that should have made up my lunch that I was giving the game away. Cyrus only mewed the louder, however, and stretched up to grab at the counter, his full body elongated to look extra lean and hungry.

With a fork, I broke up the tuna; I loosely tossed the mixture, leaving some of the fish in chunks while mixing the tiny cheese pieces throughout. I set the completed dish down on the mat and watched Cyrus dive for it. He sniffed, I waited. He sat back down, about six inches away, still facing his dish. "Dinner," his body language clearly said, "has not been served."

He didn't look at me. Didn't need to by then, his erect posture and sudden silence made my duty clear. With a sigh I pulled my jeans back on, shrugged into the sweater that already smelled like a party long gone, and reached for my boots. There would be others in the twenty-four-hour store at this hour; some buying for themselves, fulfilling the sugar or romance-deprivation whims and the late-night munchies that on a Saturday night seem reasonable. Maybe there would even be some like me, who had learned a little that night about expectations, about what you can fake and what you can demand, and how sometimes the right thing is the only thing, cheese bits and all.

To some extent we are all obsessed with our cats. On any of a dozen cat-related Internet sites, at almost any hour we discuss training and feeding, trading lore about playthings and discipline and holistic cat care. Just mention Bach's Rescue Remedy, a floral essence reputed to ease feline (and human) stress, and listen to the furor. ("It's pure quackery," one vet tells me. "But it's harmless, and some of my clients swear by it.") We spent more than $748 million on our cats in 2000, $76.2 million on toys alone, according to the American Pet Products Manufacturers Association, and even a quick browse through pet catalogs reveal the lengths to which our felines' fancies will take us. (And I say this as the proud owner of a Hammacher-Schlemmer feline drinking fountain, complete with charcoal filter.) We do this because we think we know what they want. We pamper them because we feel guilty for keeping them indoors or for neutering them. Or we do so because we want them to be happy, because we so enjoy their self-possession, their discernment—and we want both the joy of seeing them pleased and of knowing that we have pleased them.

We may, arguably, carry it too far. Would the average cat owner be willing to skin and gut a rabbit, for example? Michelle, who runs the Boston-based Blakkatz Cattery, would—and has, more than once. "It only took about a half hour," she told me as we sat with several of her American shorthairs. "And it fed everyone for several meals."

A breeder of these thickly furred, somewhat pug-faced cats, Michelle has been feeding her cats raw foods since 1993, concocting her own recipe of meat, bone meal, egg yolks, and organs from several natural-food books and the Canadian Feline Future system. Although she often substitutes human-food-quality beef or chicken for bunny, she insists on preparing the uncooked meal herself, and that means grinding the meat to a consistency that requires some chomping and chewing on the part of her domestic carnivores—the better to clean their teeth—and serving it at room temperature, for easier digestion. The result of this diet—or possibly because of the many other aspects of her loving attention—is an extremely glossy coat, as I can see on the recent mom, nursing her babies in a nearby plush cat bed.

A former farm girl, Michelle wasn't always a natural-foods fan. "I started off feeding them dry food, free-feeding them as much as they wanted." Michelle flashes back to the old days, pulling another sleek and compliant member of the cattery family onto her denim lap. When she began reading about natural diets and holistic health, her outlook turned completely around. "Cats evolved as desert creatures," she points out, explaining why such dry food is now anathema to her. "They're used to getting their water from their food. A mouse is 65 to 75 percent water." Now she focuses on foods "that are as close to prey as they can be." (In fact, a recent article in the *Journal of the American Veterinary Medical Association* [*JAVMA*] recommends a care-

fully monitored mix of good-quality commercial food supplemented by fresh foods and specifies that the fresh foods should
be cooked to avoid possible bacteriological contamination.)

Since Michelle's conversion, however, every kitten that leaves
her cattery does so only after its new owner has promised to continue the natural diet. Preparing such food, she acknowledges,
takes more time than opening a can. (The *JAVMA* article warns
that without extreme care such diets may become dangerously
unbalanced.) However, Michelle argues, the care is not onerous
and the time is amply compensated for. "I think I spend a lot less
time at the vet's office than many caretakers do. I spend less time
cleaning litter boxes and vacuuming." She strokes a glossy tabby.
"If we are going to keep such an animal we should respect its
heritage."

All of us must make our own decisions about how much we'll
indulge our cats. We must also, sometimes more consciously
than others, set limits on how much we will indulge ourselves
with cats. Because there is such a thing as too many cats. Most of
us know this. For some of us, however, the only limits have been
set by others. When these are removed, the fur can fly.

"Once I got separated and divorced, I thought, 'Now I can
have as many cats as I want!'" Sheera told me, as I toured the
rooms of the no-kill shelter that she has established in her somewhat tumble-down house. With thirty-three cats in residence
when I visited, her passion seems to know no bounds, her wiry
strength and commanding voice all focused on her cats. If it
weren't for her work with local animal control officers I would
worry about the short, muscular brunette, anxious that the
"splurge" she repeatedly fussed over (on a pair of discount jeans
for herself) and the cat budget she mentions in a much more
casual tone (approximately ten thousand dollars each year on

litter, food, and vet care) meant that such passion had given way to obsession. The transition is easier than it seems. Especially for those of us who are kind and self-supporting and often living on our own, as we find ourselves called upon to adopt first one or two pets, then those on the brink of being abandoned by friends or neighbors, and then local strays.

For Sharon, living in a one-bedroom apartment with nine cats, the situation is not ideal, but does at least provide fodder for her stand-up comedy routine. "My ex-boyfriend who I threw out of here had three cats of his own," says the Los Angeles–based comedian, who entered that relationship with her two cats, Foo Foo and Gigi. "And he would take in cats. He'd go to the pound and come back with a cat. At one point we had eleven or twelve. That's when I knew he was insane."

When the ex moved back East, he left Sharon with all the animals he'd brought home. "He just took off and didn't want to deal," recalls the petite woman, who resembles a cat herself with her diamond-shaped face and flashing eyes. Although she loves cats—"my family has always been a cat family"—she isn't that pleased to be living with so many. For now, her comedy career has been put on hold while she tries to get at least five of the pride adopted. "But it's definitely given me a few minutes of material," she notes wryly. One suspects that she would rather trade some new jokes to have her living room back.

"Did I tell you I'm allergic?" she continues. "And I have nine. I can pet them, but I can't let them in my face. That's it, it's over. I get really teary and my face itches." She still sleeps with them, "five at a time. They sleep with me in shifts." However, in the interest of breathing, the cats are otherwise shepherded out of her bedroom and into her living room or her building's courtyard.

"I'm anal about my cleaning. I vacuum every day, I get up every morning and sweep up the fur. It's a lot of work having nine cats. People think I'm insane.

"People come over and go, 'Ooh! A kitty!' Then, 'Oh, another kitty!' Then, 'Oh shit, it's another cat.' And I tell them, 'Yeah, yeah, just go on into the bedroom.' "

So how many cats are too many? For most of us the answer is a fuzzy, gray (and thus Cyrus-like) area. After all, I have stood in the homes of women—women passionately involved in cat rescue—and pondered my own limits. I have met women—and they are almost always women—who have let their houses fall into disrepair, allowed their relationships with fellow humans to slide, and seen full-time jobs go by the wayside because of the amount of time, not to mention energy and money, they have chosen to give to their feline charges. I have walked into homes that reeked of urine, where the litter boxes are changed regularly but the presence of twenty or thirty or more cats being sheltered or fostered, of ferals being tamed or protected, simply overwhelms the best efforts of their human cohabitants.

These women, whether professionals affiliated with pounds and animal hospitals or kindhearted amateurs seeking to save ferals from horrible deaths on the street, make different choices from those many of us simple pet lovers would make. For them, taking in cats is not about finding a pet to love but about helping otherwise friendless creatures. It may be a sane choice as well as a humane one; their reasoning is usually rational. They are often the pillars of their animal-rights communities. So where do we draw the line?

"I've reached my limit," says Jeanette. With twenty-one cats living in either her Washington State house or her securely fenced yard, including six ferals who will not allow human contact, she has as many as she can deal with. Living alone, she doesn't have to justify the $200 to $250 a month she spends on food and litter, but when she figures in vet bills—all her cats have regular care, including microchip identification implants—the costs begin to seem excessive, even to her. Plus, she's aware that some of her neighbors regard her as a bit odd. "When people ask how many I have, I just say, 'A bunch,' " she explains.

Jeanette loves her extended feline family. "They keep me centered," she says, and talks about how the cats seemed to take turns keeping her company after foot surgery immobilized her last year. "I don't think anybody in their right mind sets out to say, 'Oh I'm going to have twenty-one cats.' But you find them and you can't find them a home and you don't want them to be killed and you say, 'Okay, what's one more?' "

"I'd like to say no," adds Marcela, whose old country house and the attached garage is home to twenty cats, as well as five dogs and some abandoned rabbits that she is fostering. Marcela's situation began to escalate when she and her husband moved out of the city six years ago. One of their two pet cats had died and she put the word out that she was willing to adopt a stray. People began calling her and dropping off cats. "Initially, we had cats to satisfy our needs, to cuddle with," she says. "The reason I take cats in now is not because I need to take care of them, but because they need to be taken care of."

Marcela knows that she has hit—or is nearing—her limit, because she recognizes how the cats have limited her interaction with other humans. The couple live an hour outside of town, she explains, which means two hours of travel to see their old friends. "And it's easier to not go out to dinner with anybody than to feed and walk everybody first and then come home to litter boxes. I can't travel anymore either, and I used to enjoy travel."

Cat care has deeper implications for Marcela as well.

Although she has won some renown as an artist, she recognizes that her menagerie has taken time from what could be promising work. Making time to paint, however, does not always seem like the right choice. "I either have to be brutal about it and say, 'No more,' because my life is not what I want it to be," she says. "Or think, 'Well, what's another hour spent making paintings when it's an animal's life?' It's a real tug of war." Her personal life has also felt the impact of the hours of animal care. "As my relationship with my husband goes, as long as he doesn't have to deal with cleaning and feeding them, I think he doesn't care anymore."

Still, she remains haunted by the one cat that she did turn away, a feral that had tested positive for feline leukemia. "It still really bothers me," she says. "I didn't follow up and see what happened to it."

Marcela and Jeanette are not alone. I've spent hours with other women like them, such as Gayle, who adores her two pet cats—and whose basement housed thirty-seven ferals the day I came by. Or Sheera, who is applying for nonprofit status for her informal shelter. These women, and many more like them, have made conscious choices about what they will sacrifice for the animals they love. They are aware of the compromises they have made. They keep up with vet care and litter box cleaning, with feeding and neutering. For the most part, they see themselves (in Sheera's words) as "way stations," temporary refuges between permanent homes for cats that have been lost or abandoned and will once again be loved. Usually, these women are actively involved in trying to find homes for at least some of these cats. They care for so many, for the most part, not because they want two dozen or three dozen felines in their homes, but because they cannot stand the alternatives. "It's one thing when it's one or two cats," explains Marcela. "It's another when it's fifteen litter boxes. It's not fun. It's about addressing their needs."

Some people, some cat-loving women in particular, are not as clear in their thinking. They're the ones, like Marilyn Barletta of San Francisco, who spark the horror stories: In that May 2001 case, 196 cats were found living in their own filth in a two-story house she had purchased for them. Women like Barletta are the ones who take in every cat and let them breed so that generation piles up on inbred generation, and cats are found cannibalizing each other, starved and sick. These people believe they are saving the cats—Barletta reportedly considered any life preferable to euthanasia—but they don't comprehend, for some psychological reason they can't grasp, the realities of care, the necessity of neutering, of vaccinations and sanitation. "All of a sudden there were more and more cats," Barletta told the *San Francisco Chronicle*; she had started with two a few years earlier. They are the ones who have taken in cats and been unable to keep up, so that their own health and that of their putative pets is endangered by feces and bacteria and often as well by the unburied corpses of some poor ignored felines. At least six such bodies were found in Barletta's care; at least one had been partially eaten by its starving housemates.

Cat "collecting" or *hoarding*, as such behavior is termed by professionals, is a mysterious phenomenon, one on which studies have only recently begun. Gary Patronek, director of the Center for Animals and Public Policy at Tufts University Veterinary Medical School, is one of the few national experts helping unravel the sad mystery. The difference between an animal lover and a hoarder, he explains, is not number of animals, but awareness—a realistic grasp of the level of care necessary and of both human and feline quality of life. The Web site of

Patronek's group, the Hoarding of Animals Research Consortium, defines a hoarder as "someone who accumulates a large number of animals; fails to provide minimal standards of nutrition, sanitation and veterinary care; and fails to act on the deteriorating condition of the animals (including disease, starvation and even death) or the environment (severely overcrowded and unsanitary conditions), or the negative impact of the collection on their own health and well-being."

These are not simply overenthusiastic cat lovers. In one study, published in the *Psychiatric Times*, Patronek looked at data from fifty-four cases, obtained from a survey of animal shelter operators: Dead or sick animals were found in 80 percent of the reported cases. In 69 percent, animal feces and urine were found in the hoarder's living areas, and more than 25 percent of the hoarders' beds were soiled by their animals. But the problem wasn't simply in keeping up with their wayward pets: According to Patronek's findings, nearly 60 percent of the hoarders would not, or could not, acknowledge that they had any problems with their animals or level of animal care.

Cats, his study found, aren't the only animals that get hoarded, simply the most common. (Dog hoarding follows close behind, although these are primarily hoarded by men.) About 65 percent of all cases involve cats, however, and Patronek estimates that there are seven hundred to two thousand new cases of animal hoarding every year in the United States.

This odd syndrome, Patronek and other animal- and mental-health experts say, may be a manifestation of obsessive-compulsive disorder (OCD), an anxiety disorder that causes those suffering from it to limit their lives through fears and rituals. According to the National Institute of Mental Health (NIMH), more than 2 percent of the population suffers from obsessive-compulsive disorder, and (according to a survey by

Randy Frost and the NIMH) 15 to 30 percent of those OCD sufferers experience hoarding of some sort as their primary symptom. With this in mind, some therapists of hoarders are prescribing antianxiety drugs, such as Paxil, to quell their patients' irrational needs.

It is interesting to note, however, that according to the *Diagnostic and Statistical Manual of Mental Disorders*, the codification Bible of mental illnesses great and small, obsessive-compulsive disorder is evenly divided between men and women. Cat hoarding, however, is much more of a women's problem. Patronek's study found that most of the hoarders (76 percent) were women. Almost half of these women lived alone, as Marilyn Barletta did. Almost half were elderly; Barletta was sixty-one.

As with pet lovers, the reasons for the hoarding run the gamut. Hoarders, Patronek's reports say, often describe an intense love for their cats. They view their cats as surrogate family. And they take in more cats because they fear for the animals out on their own, not realizing that they may be endangering them all the more by trapping them in an untenable situation. The gap between what they perceive and what is really happening is terrifying and, for some animals, deadly.

There are only nineteen cats the day I visit "Connie" (not her real name) on the suggestion of a local shelter worker. Only, that is, down from a recent twenty-five, before the predations of some local coyotes. This is before the arrival of the three from Maine that are being dropped off by a concerned cat lover who knows that their owner, a visiting professor, is returning to Europe without them.

Only one cat greets me, a gray tiger who looks both glossy and well fed as he rubs against my ankles. I have already circled the house, a big, shambling summer cottage, but could find no doorbell on any of the three doors. As I stood back, considering the closed-off porch, the little tiger found me, and, stepping back after his friendly greeting, leads me without hesitation to one dark entrance on the side of the house. It is dinnertime, clearly, and the late-autumn afternoon is growing both cold and increasingly wet. I knock and we are both welcomed in by the equally compact, somewhat stout, gray-haired woman who has brought all these cats together.

Once inside, I get a better sense of what the shelter worker had warned me about. Although we are in New England, on the last day of October, flies buzz about as if it were midsummer. In the drafty chill, the odor of litter box is not too bad, but the dry food spilling off the cats' big serving platter crunches underfoot. And everywhere, everywhere, there are cats. "This is Radcliffe," she introduces me to a large black-and-white longhair curled regally on the kitchen counter. "And here's Buzzy." A small orange adolescent skims by my legs. On the stove top—the kind with flat electric burners—a marmalade longhair turns and looks at us, scratches for fleas, and then curls his legs under him to nap. Connie ushers me off to the right, to a small sitting room where four more cats sleep or recline on a sofa; another darts up the stairs.

"This is Ashley, and here's his brother." Connie reaches around a cushion to scoop up the siblings of the marmalade longhair on the oven, the other now-adult littermates who share the luxuriant orange-and-white fur. Holding the compliant bundles we retire back to the kitchen. There was one more in that litter, Connie tells me, settling into one of the few unoccupied chairs. Her voice grows harder. Drunks killed her, she says.

"I heard them out there, drinking and throwing bottles." Connie and her husband live down a dirt road, but their woods are surrounded by suburb and it is easy to see how a woman like Connie could come to be the local scapegoat, the entertainment for rowdy teens. "I found her in the morning," Connie continues. "She was slit open."

More than coyotes prey on the cat lady's cats: People fear what they do not understand. Even I, a cat lover, remember the frisson of nervousness as I circled her dark house in search of a lighted door, and the faint hope that she would not—even after our phone conversation—let me in. Not all her neighbors are cruel, however. Some, such as the couple who called the Society for the Prevention of Cruelty to Animals to investigate the elderly couple's feline haven, have the welfare of the animals in mind.

Not that Connie sees the intervention in quite that light. "They stole my cat," she protests, allowing the shaggy orange-and-white to jump down from her lap as she turns again to the cat on the counter behind her. She had thought this cat, Radcliffe, had gone missing and for days searched the neighborhood for signs of his black-and-white bulk. She spotted him, finally, sitting in the window of a neighbor's house, but when she was able to confront the people there later that day, they seemed nonplussed by her outrage. "We're going to adopt him," they told her, informing her that they had already taken the animal to the vet. "You can't do that. He's my cat!" Connie had replied, and after paying the vet's bill—two hundred dollars to treat an abscess— she had taken him home. That's when the ASPCA was called, and the inspector ("who was very polite," Connie notes) began coming around.

He told her he was there to inquire about why she had not taken the cat for his follow-up treatment, to remove the wick that the vet was using to drain the deep infected wound on the cat's head. "I told him that I've been taking care of cats all my life"; she seems affronted by the memory. "I pulled it out, and it healed cleanly." Her cats are all spayed or neutered, she says, but after that she sees no need for a vet, especially one who charges "Saks Fifth Avenue prices."

Over several visits he could find no reason to remove her cats, she tells me proudly. I make the mental note that he must have been looking for more obvious signs of abuse or neglect. She has even recently switched from supermarket brands to the healthier Iams food, although she complains about the prices. "I'm feeding them less these days," she confides in me, her voice lowering. "So there's less waste."

Maybe the inspector had been told the same story I had, the one that made me nervous about seeking her out that afternoon. "She thought one of her cats was lost," a shelter worker who had befriended her had told me. "She looked everywhere for him." Two weeks later, the friend told me, the missing pet had been found dead, trapped behind Connie's husband's bed. "Couldn't you tell?" the friend had asked. "Well, you know me and housekeeping," was Connie's reply.

It was that story I'd been thinking of as I followed the directions up the rutted road, and although I anticipated the smell and the disarray, I didn't expect the sadness. First, as any experience with a cat hoarder makes clear, because of the condition of the cats (although the ones I see seem reasonably well fed despite their scratches and scars). Sad also because as Connie's perhaps mild case makes clear, those who hoard have no concept of the mistreatment to which they are subjecting their cats. Although these women are clearly the basis for much anticat bias, they suffer without understanding. These are the women who gave our society the image of the witch: the "crazy cat ladies" who are ostracized and isolated to a degree that must surely aggravate their mental states. To women like Connie, those calls to the animal inspector were a personal attack on her family. The possibility that Radcliffe might have been better off with a family of his own, two people to love him as their house pet, could not be imagined.

Cats had always been around during Connie's childhood. Indeed the question of when she got her first cat seems to surprise her. I've always had cats, she tells me. But these first pets, under the supervision of her mother and father, came singly into her life. "One cat at a time," she says, although that cat would often be supplemented by a dog or another pet in their Manhattan apartment. "When I got married, I thought, I can finally have all the cats I want." As a newlywed living in Paris, she began with two Siamese. Fifty-three years later, she hasn't satisfied that craving yet. She still wants more, and nobody is stopping her.

How does her husband feel about the animals here? I ask her, not wanting to mention the shelter worker's story. "He's out of his gourd," she responds, and I think she means over the cats. "He's a grump. But when I get the cats he doesn't want me to give them away. He just doesn't want any new ones. After all, I'm the one feeding the cats. I sit and look at television and clean the cats' ears."

"He's half-assed," she says again later, when I ask her again about her husband of five decades. "Like this house. We bought it for the cats," she explains. "It was a summer cottage and he never finished insulating it. A half-assed job. It's cold; it's always cold." Her home does have some heat, so she does not fall into the significant percentage of cat hoarders with nonfunctional utilities. But it is drafty this afternoon and as we sit there, she pulls her sweater around her. I point out the cat curled on the table beside her. "These fellows must keep you warm," I say. "I sleep with five of them," she replies. "With the five who won't wake me up."

Her husband, Bob, makes his way slowly down the stairs.

"Too many cats," he calls out to me. Since he's now nearly deaf, Connie had yelled an explanation of my project to him. "Too many cats!" he repeats in the overloud voice of the hearing impaired. He shakes my hand and walks out.

I find myself sympathizing with the old man, as much as with his wife. Do I want to meet the five who live in her bedroom? No, I tell her, I cannot. It is getting dark, I say. It is getting late and I would like to get back to the city before traffic becomes unbearable. In truth, the claustrophobia of the small kitchen and adjoining parlor has begun to get to me and I do not want to enter a smaller space, particularly where more cats live exclusively. I begin to make my farewells, but Connie doesn't acknowledge them. Instead, she pulls a homemade calendar off the wall. Each month boasts a picture of a different cat, several of the ones I have met and also some of those that have been killed. There are Mermaid and Gray Stray and Priscilla, found on the rocks at Priscilla Beach. There is Adolph, "because of his mustache," she says, flipping to another month, and Duxbury. "The coyote got him." Lovely, I respond as the photos begin to repeat, and start to move toward the door. She follows, with more photos, and I can do nothing else but look and praise the somewhat blurry shots of cats living and dead. "This is Hawthorne," she says. The black-and-white in the photo is clearly labeled as Radcliffe. "He's three years old." She has already told me his age, which is nearly three times that. We reach the end of the photos and I walk out the door. It is raining and windy by then, but she follows me, wearing only her cardigan.

Did I see the cat cemetery? She points out a circular area right off the driveway, bordered by stones and with many larger stones that seem to serve as markers. "More than thirty of my babies are here," she says. I mutter something that I hope sounds comforting and pull my keys from my pocket. The wind has picked up and it is almost fully dark. I reach my hand out to take hers. "Good-bye," I say. "You won't make it back to Boston," she replies, and I wait for her to finish, to say "by sunset" or "before rush hour." She doesn't. "Well," I say with a laugh, feigning a jauntiness I do not feel, "I will eventually!" I fairly dive into my Toyota and drive down the unpaved road much faster than is good for my suspension. Although she has my sympathy, it is dark and stormy and it is also Halloween. For the fifty miles home, I clutch the steering wheel tightly and ride the brake on every turn.

8

LITTERING

"How's my little pussums?" I ask Cyrus, as I scoop him into my arms, cradling his hindquarters with one forearm while positioning him against my shoulder. "Would we like a little turkey?" I'm using my baby-talk voice, and it's either my unabashed cutesy approach or the way I'm holding the cat against my body that makes my friend Lisa comment: "You know, that's another aspect of the woman-cat relationship." Lisa has two herself. "Cyrus weighs about as much as a human baby, and . . ." I interrupt her. "Yes, I know, but a baby wouldn't be covered with soft gray fur."

Or arrive trained to use a litter box, I might have added. Or be capable of fending for himself if left alone for hours or even days with a bowl of crunchies and another of fresh water.

However, I can't really blame Lisa. The idea that for many women, particularly single and childless women, a cat replaces an infant is an old one. The comparable weight, size, and apparent cuddliness of cats and babies give strength to this theory, as does our tendency to spoil—that is "to baby"—our feline darlings as perhaps we would a child. Much has also been made of the infantlike features of cats: the wide-set eyes, relatively flat face, and round cheeks, as well as the high-pitched mewling cries that supposedly stir our maternal instincts, no matter how latent. That doesn't mean we have to enjoy the comparison.

"I always objected to that comparison, to people who tell me that I treat my cats like my children," says Lauren, "but I have to say there's some truth to it." A recent fire alarm proved the point to the young artist. Caught alone in the studio she shares with her boyfriend, she immediately reached for her two cats. Butler she quickly urged into his carrier, but the scared, skinny Ezra she couldn't push into his box. And so she froze, unable to leave without both her pets. Luckily, the alarm proved to be false. "I was standing on the fire escape, crying and holding Ezra, and utterly unable to move. Afterward, people told me, 'You were holding that cat just like a baby,' and they were right.

"I guess any physical contact can be pleasurable and can make that connection strong," Lauren concludes, and I agree. There's nothing wrong with physical affection, giving or receiving, however you get it. What makes the theories linking cat love and baby love offensive is that outsiders seem to suppose our ignorance of the difference. Although we are as powerfully moved by instinct as the next mammal, we are not brainless hormone receptors, gravitating to the nearest infant-sized creature with the insatiable desire to hold it to our breast. We are, for the most part, clearly aware of our desire to love something, if not someone. And sometimes, just sometimes, we have made a choice and actually prefer a pet to a child. A cat will not outlive us, in all likelihood, nor carry our family name into the next millennium. But, in addition to all the reasons listed previously, a cat may be otherwise preferable. A cat will never crash the car or break our hearts with drugs or alcohol or really bad relationship choices. We're talking a smaller return on a smaller investment, but in a life that may already be filled with demands on our time, energy, and heart, there is often at least room for the love and fulfillment that comes from the cuddling of a cat.

For many of us, our cats came along at times when we could not have, or would not have wanted to have, children. Many of us were newly fledged adults when we got our cats. Out of college, working, living alone or in apartments shared with virtual strangers as we began to make our ways in the world, we were just beginning to determine our own lives, and our cats were, in some ways, the first companions we got to choose. We had been freed from the restrictions of dorm life or of our parents' homes. We were learning to cook and to care for ourselves, and one of our first moves was to get a cat. We probably could not afford all our own furniture—we decorated instead with familial castoffs, gifts, and some careful trash picking—but we could afford those cans of Friskies. We worked too hard, kept hours that were too long to include motherhood. And most of us were single, still trying to figure out adult social lives: how to date and mate and balance relationships with what we hoped were burgeoning careers. But we wanted to come home at night to warmth. A purr and smooth brush against the calf often meant a lot after climbing four flights of stairs simply to unlock a cold dark studio with kitchenette.

Even later on, when some of us have sorted through those issues of work and love and insufficient apartment space, many of us still do not have children. However, we all need to love, to love something warm and sentient that responds in some way to our demonstrations of affection. Some of us are meant to be mothers; some make that choice with surety, some on faith. Others of us do not get the opportunity, and still others of us are childless by choice. Those of us who are childless are not always without regret; we may have complicated feelings about our families and about parenting, or have an interest in nurturing young people in different ways. But these decisions and opportunities, or their lack, do not diminish or make less worthy our love of cats. For those of us who have bonded with these beautiful creatures, the companionship we enjoy with them is real. The warmth we feel when we stare into their mystical gold or green or blue eyes is real. The solace we receive when stroking their deep fur is real, and love of any kind, nurturing of any kind, must surely be respected. Our love, our capacity for caring, enriches us, no matter what the world thinks of the objects of our affection.

"When I tell people I have cats rather than children, they go, 'How eccentric!' " notes Kyoko, a Japanese-born novelist who cohabits with two Siamese. "It's always derogatory." Sometimes, as many of us know, what the world thinks can be hurtful in subtle ways. We internalize the sneers and wonder too often if our cat-love makes us incapable of baby-love. "I'm always hearing about that lonely old-lady-with-the-cat thing," adds Laura, another single cat lover. "I'm going to be one of those old ladies, living with ten cats," she explains, as if this were necessarily bad.

What we are facing is a prejudice that implies that babies and cats are somehow antithetical. Even if we no longer believe the hateful rumors—the so-called "old wives' tales" that were in reality probably fostered by men, which claimed that cats would seek to kill our babies—we can still be shaken by the negative associations such tales engender. We may internalize them and make ourselves susceptible to worry over imagined unfitness, fearing that we love our cats "too much" or instead of children. We begin to accept the rumormongers' fallacy that love is a finite resource.

The strongest of us are content with our choices and I count myself lucky to be talking these over with a woman like Kyoko. Algernon, one of her two pets, has already risen to check me out, his long wedge-shaped nose nearly snuffling, when the Japanese-American writer comes back with our tea. "Meh," he says quietly, for a Siamese. "Meh." Having had his say, the brown sealpoint settles back in with his bluepoint flatmate, Ernest, and lets his woman talk.

"My mother had a cat when I was born," begins Kyoko, tucking her legs beneath her as we wait for the tea to steep. "There are no pictures of the cat, because the cat didn't like cameras, but I've been told we got along just fine. She slept with me. So I was imprinted early."

That cat died while Kyoko was still an infant, and many catless years followed. The affinity was only reawakened by coincidence, when a roommate's sister dumped her two, Mabel and Angus, in Kyoko's shared college-town apartment. "We weren't supposed to have pets, but she had nowhere else to place them." Angus, a diminutive all-black male, quickly won the young writer's heart. "He had a great personality," she says, her face lighting up over the steam of the tea. "I loved him."

After two months, however, those cats moved on, placed in a permanent home by their original owner. Kyoko was despondent. "I talked to my roommates about it." The landlord didn't seem to care. But the two men she shared the apartment with were not interested. "I said, 'I'll do the dishes all the time.' Which I did anyway," she points out. That did it, and soon Kyoko adopted Dorian, her first Siamese. When she caught the roommates trying to get her cat high, exhaling marijuana smoke into his long Asian face, she lost the roommates. Kyoko and Dorian struck out on their own.

For Kyoko, now in her mid-forties, Dorian was what Cyrus is

to me: the cat of her first adulthood. Dorian isn't the model for the blue-eyed white charmer in her first novel, *Stone Field, True Arrow*. That cat was based on one she met at an artist's colony. But with Dorian, a slightly chubby sealpoint, Kyoko learned to live on her own. With Dorian she married, and with Dorian she parted from her husband and built a friendship in the ashes. "My husband really loved that cat," she says, brushing back a strand of hair that has escaped from her ponytail. "We talked about the cat all the time." The marriage lasted eleven years; Dorian eighteen. When her plump cross-eyed favorite died, she says, "It was the saddest thing. It was like a postscript to my divorce. I didn't think my ex-husband and I would ever talk again."

Knowing that Dorian had lived a full and long life, Kyoko was able to grieve and move on, much as she has from her marriage. She and her ex-husband, Chuck, have found other topics to discuss, she says, much as she has found other romances and creative projects. The one creative act Kyoko hasn't felt motivated to try is childbirth.

"I never gravitated toward babies," she begins to explain. "I thought, maybe when I'm around thirty it will begin to kick in, but it never did. When I see human babies, I think, 'Why can't they be furry?' I don't like the way babies smell. I like the way cats smell." I dip my face to the fur of the two cats beside me: Algernon and Ernest have the warm smell of old leather—or clean cats.

"When my friends have new babies, I don't care much. But when my friends have new cats, I can't wait to see them!" she says. On the couch beside me, the two cats have begun to groom each other, Algernon's growly purr drowning out Ernest's quieter thrumming as Kyoko relates a story about a cross-country airplane trip taken when she was thirty-five. Seated next to her were a mother and infant, but Kyoko's early fears about wailing and wetting were soon allayed. The baby was perfectly behaved. "And I thought, 'What a nice baby! This makes me want to see my cats!'" She hides her face in her hand as she laughs at her own reaction. But when she looks up again, her bright eyes crinkled with merriment, she is smiling broadly. "To me, a baby would be a cat substitute."

For many of us like Kyoko, children will never replace cats and that's just fine. We agree, echoing a conversation that I've since had with many cat women, that living with a cat is more like having a relationship with an adult friend. Or like living with an interesting roommate whose first language isn't English. If you're looking for a child substitute, suggests Robin, who has pets of several sorts, try a dog. Dogs, points out the Los Angeles–based editor (who also loves her two pooches), are really more like kids in terms of the attention they require.

"You can't leave a dog for a day," she says. "And it looks to you for a different kind of feedback." Because cats are more independent, we agree, they seem more mature. A cat can amuse itself, and often prefers its own pursuits to yours, for example. A cat may look to you for food, but he or she will take care of his or her own bathroom and cleaning needs, for the most part. Plus, we concur, much of the joy of being with a cat is in trying to decipher its inner life. You can have a real conversation with a cat, and when it is over, you can both part with a complete sense of self, for a little while.

All of which shoots holes in the theory that we look to cats to be our substitute babies. If anything, I am realizing, at times we may seek parenting from our cats—or at least view them as sources of comfort and remembrance. Remember Linus and his blanket? The smart, quiet kid in Charles Schulz's *Peanuts* was for some of us the real hero of the comic strip. Unlike the supposed star, Charlie Brown, whose gullibility kept him innocent, and thus supposedly sympathetic, Linus was a lot more aware. He was into philosophy, and he knew what was up with the other kids in the sandlot, who in their rivalries, jealousies, and power plays represented the adult world in miniature. He understood everything going on around him, and, perhaps because he saw it all so clearly, he was the one who—long out of the crib—couldn't quite let go of his baby blanket, dragging the dirty, mangled remnant everywhere. Now that's a figure I can relate to. He is also Lucy's kid brother, a youngest child—as I am. And even though he is generally much more adult than his fiery, and often cruel, sister, he has his one soft spot. His vulnerability, his addiction to his blanket, is a perfect example of what is usually called a transitional object.

The concept, coined by D. W. Winnicott around 1951, is that a transitional object is something that helps us get used to the idea that our parents will not always be there. As infants, to take it down to its basics, we see our parents leave. Having no experience with continuity, and having scant experience with life at all, we are terrified that they will not come back to care for us and that we will perish. But often before they left, they tucked us in, perhaps making sure we had a nice cuddly teddy bear or fluffy blankie to hold on to. And hold on to it we did, for dear life, as the last remnant of safety and proof of their love, until they returned again. Ultimately, we learned to use this object to comfort ourselves as we ventured into the world, grasping onto it as a reminder of the security left behind. The scarier the situation, the more likely we were to revert to that object. In an ideal life, we would eventually learn that we did not need the transitional object. Most of us, I suspect, never quite reach this phase.

I think it likely that for many of us, myself included, pets serve as transitional objects. Like Linus's security blanket, they are warm and comforting. They help us feel in control of the world, remind us that we are loved, or have been loved, and promise us that love will once again enfold us. In that way, we are more like the babies of our cats than like their parents. They hold for us the promise of other creatures to love, acting as furry bookmarks in our hearts.

I thought of transitional objects this morning while I was writing my mother about the status of a blanket, a glorious golden brown, utterly soft throw she gave me only a few years ago. Maternal associations aside, it's a perfect match for me in color and in texture, and has won a permanent place on the back of my sofa, where I can pull it over my feet while watching television, or wrap it around my shoulders when I sit writing and the old house around me gets drafty. In the last year or so, it has also become known as Cyrus's blanket, because as much as I love its luxurious light weave, its incredible warmth, I could never respond to it as my cat has.

There was, at first, a bit of a disappointment. I had thought, you see, that Cyrus loved to knead my lap, to push and push at my admittedly cushiony thigh until he felt it was right, and then climb onto me for a nap on a cold evening. We used to time him, expecting him to show up just in time for the *Law and Order* repeats to which I am addicted. There's a song by the band Morphine that repeats the refrain: "Every night at eleven, I go out." For us, it was every night at eleven, he comes in—to the living room—and although it never quite scanned we'd sing that to him as he appeared, like clockwork, ready to knead my lap. Or so it seemed, until one warm night I pushed the blanket off my lap, but did not, as I usually do, rearrange it in its decorative but inaccessible place on the back of the sofa. As I sat there, piled-up blanket next to me, I saw my kitty saunter into the living room, pause and jump to the sofa beside me. Once there, instead of

starting to work, ears slightly back, on my flesh, he began kneading the blanket, and purring as loudly as I had ever heard him. I
did not appear to him, I realized then, the sine qua non of laps. I
had simply fulfilled the role of purveyor of blankie, and that cozy
cover was the nightly treat that made my cat whirr like a Geiger
counter.

Was the blanket his substitute for the mother long gone, or
simply a comfortable place to rest? I can't tell. Nor can I really
judge what he means to me. I can now freely admit that I was
never a doll girl. Animals, stuffed or live, were always my play-
mates of choice when I was young enough to act out openly the
fantasies of how life should be. So I don't recall ever having the
reportedly common fantasy of teaching my dolls how to take
care of their doll babies. But watching Cyrus knead his blanket,
even though I suspect that his motives are comfort and warmth,
just melts my heart. He's hunkered down in the loose, golden
weave now. Otherwise I'd just want to pick him up and hug him
and cover him with big smushy kisses. Which, some theorists
would say, just goes to prove something.

Before we jump to any conclusions here, let me state the obvious. Any pet can elicit some of the same feelings that a child
would, not the least of which is confidence in our own ability to
care for a smaller dependent creature. Often, because we love
our cats, we find ourselves in situations that may seem parental.
Leanne, for example, is learning about issues of custody and care
thanks to the two cats that she and her husband adopted. Still in
her twenties, Leanne talks about her marriage in rather vague
phrases, generalizing about what went right—"we're still on
good terms"—and what didn't—"basically, I just chose to leave

the relationship." But the young marketing professional is very clear about how they both wanted to protect their kitties, Abigail and Dallas.

"We didn't want to traumatize the cats," explains Leanne, introducing her "big boy," the black-and-white Dallas, and his more delicate calico housemate. "So, at first, we agreed to let my husband keep them in the apartment where we both had lived." Leanne had moved into a small one-bedroom flat nearby, but enjoyed visitation privileges. "He traveled a lot and so I was always visiting them and taking care of them," she says. When her ex decided to move, the two were forced to reconfigure their responsibilities. Again, the cats came first. Her apartment, they both agreed, was clearly too small for one adult and two cats, particularly the fifteen-pound Dallas. "So we worked out a deal," Leanne explains. "I moved back into the apartment where we had lived together for the benefit of the cats. And he helps me out on the rent—for the benefit of the cats."

Clearly, some of what we have learned from our cats may be transferred to the care of children, if we choose to have them. "I don't have kids yet, but we're trying," Ellen says with hope, and a bit of nervousness. "I have definitely learned a lot about patience from my cats. I have a tendency to be overprotective, and I'm sure I still will be," says the adoptive mother of Wilbur and the late Kitty. "But I've learned not to take offense, to not take it personally if the cat doesn't want to be petted. I think it will translate."

According to Louise, much of our cat caring does carry over. "Spike taught me about parenting," says Louise, a tall blonde with a deep, calm voice. A year after her cat's death, the Ohio native recalls her feisty black-and-white pet fondly. "She trained me to be a good mother."

In some ways, Louise explains, Spike helped her grow into a conscious, responsible adult, one who was capable of taking care of herself as well as one small cat. As is true for so many of us, Spike came into Louise's life soon after she graduated college. A friend's cat had kittens and one tiny tuxedoed kitten proved irresistible to the young professional, a brilliant student who felt somewhat adrift in the real world.

"When I was living by myself, Spike and I had a really intense relationship," recalls Louise, sipping tea in the hundred-and-fifty-year-old house she and her husband are renovating. "She was one of the few significant beings in my life. I could make myself cry thinking about her death. I just could not bear it." She pauses to remember those lonely days, before Jim, before her son, Christian, and even before the circle of friends and colleagues that now sustains her.

"I thought at the time that it was like contemplating the death of a child. I wouldn't make that comparison now." She draws an outline on the table with one finger. "When you don't have children, your cat is like your child. When you have a child, that relationship is so much more intense and complicated. Your relationship with your spouse changes too," she notes. "It changes all of your nerve endings.

"But I feel like I had hints of that in caring for Spike. I was not very good at caring for her at first. I didn't change the litter often enough. I remember finding maggots in her food," she grimaces, her usual reserve disappearing for a moment.

"She needed me: she would have starved to death if I hadn't fed her. She was a dependent creature. I think I resisted that for a long time." The relaxed woman sitting across from me barely resembles the young Yale graduate, for whom such mundanities as buying groceries or paying taxes seemed overwhelming. "It wasn't until Spike that I started learning how to take care of myself and started taking care of another creature."

That tutoring grew intense during the last few months of Spike's life, when the small cat's kidneys began to fail and Louise opted to hydrate her with a nightly subcutaneous drip. "I wouldn't have had the patience to do the drip for her when I first adopted her, but I got much better at that kind of task." She is clearly recalling the last months when, after she put Christian to bed, she'd hold the weakened, ailing Spike on her lap. How those round eyes would look up at her calmly as she stroked the smooth black back and watched the saline solution run under her skin. "When you're in the mode of constantly taking care of another being, it doesn't seem like that big a deal.

"I needed to learn that and Spike taught me," she says quietly, thinking back. "They are living creatures, and they remind us that living creatures have needs and that we are creatures too. For someone who grew up living in her head, that was a lesson I needed to learn."

"We always regarded the cats as Alice's aunts and uncles," says Suford, who raised her only child in a house full of cats, at one point as many as twelve. "They would watch her, and it was clear to me after a while that they showed her things and she learned. Some of it had to do with attitude, and some of it had to do with actual things she learned from watching them, like climbing over the child gate. They took a benign and friendly interest in her."

Suford, whose grown daughter is now helping readers like me in a Harvard Square comic-book store, is a jolly older woman, her long brown hair shot with gray. The cats, she says, helped her develop a sense of ease with the baby. "We wanted to keep

Alice in the bed with us. It was just easier, and it seemed nice. And she was six and a half pounds when she was born, about the size of a small cat. We'd had the cats in bed with us and we'd never rolled on them or crushed them, and that gave us a little confidence with Alice."

Suford and her husband, Tony, checked with their pediatrician, and soon the entire extended family was sharing a bed—including the cats. Suford had heard the tales, of course, the ones that claim that cats kill babies. "We asked about the old stories," she says, mentioning the horrid myth that cats smother infants by covering their faces or by "stealing their breath." "But cats don't sit on babies," says Suford, clearly miffed at such silliness. "The cats sniff babies and may want to cuddle next to them. They're curious, of course."

Not that the cats, Suford recalls, were always impressed by their young protégé. "We were all sitting in bed reading and relaxing before going to sleep," the tall lean woman remembers. "Alice was a few months old and crawling around on the bed. The cats were sitting at the foot of the bed watching her progress. Then they looked at me, at each other, then back to me. I could not have heard them more plainly if they had had the full power of speech! 'Oh, isn't it too bad,' they said, dripping with a smug superior pretense of sympathy, 'that her kitten is so retarded.' After all, at three months kittens are much more fully coordinated and able." Suford did not try to explain the difference to the two tabbies. They would only have pitied her more.

Clearly, motherhood does not need to rule out cat love, any more than it does a professional career. Not that we should be careless: There may be some risk to pregnant women and the children they carry from cat's feces. Hunting cats can pick up the microscopic parasite *Toxoplasma gondii* from such prey as mice and birds, and those parasites can lay eggs that get passed in their feces. Women who handle infected waste are in danger of picking up the parasite and infecting themselves and their babies with the disease it carries, known as toxoplasmosis, which can cause blindness and hearing loss as well as other problems for congenitally infected children. Because of this risk, pregnant women and those with compromised immune systems should avoid changing litter, just as they should probably not eat raw meat or sushi. But considering that one-third of the adult populations of the United States and Europe already carry antibodies to the parasite (according to the American Veterinary Medical Association), this seems a minor worry—a cause for caution, certainly, but not a reason to shed a pet.

Nor should mothers-to-be worry overmuch about behavioral problems. A new child is a source of stress, as well as joy, for the entire family, of course. But as Suford's story illustrates, cats may welcome a new baby. In fact, aggressive behavior by a cat toward a new child is extremely rare: An American Animal Hospital Association survey reports that of all pet owners (including dog owners) only 13 percent of the ones who say their pet has ever exhibited *any* jealous behavior report that the jealousy has been directed toward a new baby or child.

The mix of motherhood and cat love comes up when Melissa, our vet and a new mother, drops by. She's just given Cyrus his latest round of shots and he's fled the room, but as I make out a check for her house call, she shows me a picture of her red tabby Finnegan sprawled beneath baby Sydney's walker. "The amount of attention I give Finnegan has probably decreased, but I still adore him," Melissa says, flipping to more recent photos of her ten-month-old daughter and eleven-year-old cat. "If anything, he's endeared himself to me more because he's so good with her. I can tolerate his disgusting behavior more—he sprays—because he's so good with her. He's never bit her or scratched her; he's a real laid-back cat and he likes to be around her. When she was really small, when Sydney was crying, Finnegan would run around in circles, like he was telling me, 'You'd better help her!' "

The affection, says the vet, is mutual. "When I go, 'Where's the kitty-kitty?' Sydney looks for him. And when he comes into the room, she gets all excited."

Through Finnegan, Melissa is teaching her daughter proper behavior around animals. "She'll still grab his hair. But if I say, 'Be gentle,' she'll let go. When I say, 'Pat nice,' she doesn't always know what to do, but she doesn't scream or cry." Melissa calls herself the "visiting vet" and makes house calls to cats all over the Greater Boston area. "I took Sydney on a couple of calls when she was really little, and she loved the little kitty-cats we'd see."

"There's your first cat lady," she says of her daughter, going back to that shot of Sydney smiling as Finnegan stretches out his full orange length beneath her.

Not all her clients integrate their loves so well. "You do see a lot of women who have a baby and ditch their cats," says the compact blonde, now squatting on the floor to gather her stethoscope and bag. "I understand that more now that I have a kid: A lot of the emotion you put into your cats you're now putting into a human. Some of it is that women are too damned tired. It's the baby first, then the husband, then themselves—and the cat falls off the radar screen.

"But I have some clients who just want to get rid of their cats," she says, her temper coloring her pale cheeks. "They say, 'Oh, the cat started scratching. I think the baby's allergic. I can't be bothered.' It really pisses me off," she says. "Finnegan's the love of my life," she concludes, and heads out the door.

At some point, Tish taught me, our cats may come to replace children, at least as our constant charges. We're talking on a plane ride, this divorced mother of two and I. She's a slim blonde, an academic who lives out in the suburbs with her two teenagers, as different from me as I can imagine, and we're both pleased to have found some common ground. Cats really do bring women together, we agree, over club sodas and airplane pretzels. She tells me that last spring, when she and her husband separated ("It was a good thing, really," she says) she thought, "Well, I have the dog and the cat." Then her dog developed a terminal illness, and soon after that her cat was mauled during a brief outing. After one expensive surgery, the family resigned itself to euthanasia, and soon after, Tish and her kids brought home two tiger kittens, Rudy and Gigi, sisters from a shelter litter. "It's nice to come home and have the cats there," she says. "It doesn't feel as lonely."

"I was just kind of living in the moment," she looks back. "Trying to fill the void." Then, sometime during the past winter, it hit her. Her son and daughter are both in high school, fourteen and sixteen years old, respectively; they're young adults developing their own lives. "The kittens," she says with a trace of midwestern twang, "are not even a year old. They'll be here with me long after my kids are grown and gone."

🐾

"They *are* my kids," says Iris. A professional breeder of the silky-coated Turkish Angoras and the densely furred, serious-looking Russian blues, Iris has the high cheekbones and bright coloring of an Angora. Her cheeks pinken and her dark eyes light up as she declares her affection for the miniature champions that scamper around her roomy duplex. "I love them all."

As we talk, one of her grand champions—Willy (or Wild Fire,

according to her papers) has begun kneading my lap. She soon settles down, her cameo (to use the show term) or salt-and-pepper head tucked into her silver-and-white tail.

For the two kittens bouncing off the furniture around us, the show life of a purebred has already started. Since so many traits skip a generation, Iris explains, the record of a cat's grandparents is often considered more important than how his or her parents did. Behavior and demeanor can win or lose points as well, which is why as soon as the kittens are born the training kicks in.

In her twelve years as a breeder, Iris has seen hundreds of litters, both of the short-haired Russians her late husband favored and her personal choice, the less popular Turks. Like most breeders, she will usually only keep one from a litter.

Most of the time, Iris admits, a breeder will pick out the kitten that best embodies the desirable traits of each breed. Professionalism counts more than sentiment, but when you're lucky, both come together.

"I knew Willie was gorgeous at birth," she says, talking about the silky creature purring in my lap. The Angora's delicate bone structure, Iris says, was apparent "while she was still wet."

Usually, identifying the star of the litter takes several weeks, if not months, and so each potential champion must be trained for the ring. Training begins with the kind of handling that makes any kitten a well-socialized pet. This means lots of strokes and lap time, ideally by friends and neighbors as well as the breeder, because new hands accustom the kitten to the many strangers it will meet at shows. After the first week, Iris will begin picking the cats up, holding their lengthening bodies in both hands as a judge will to check the slim muscular bodies' contours. By the time they're weaned, the kittens will be as comfortable being stretched out in midair as they are with nursing. To complete their training, the kittens get a full round of interactive play—

chasing feathers and bouncy toys much like a judge will display—and taking trips. A show cat has to travel and has to be calm under any circumstance. "I take my kittens to the pet supply market," says Iris. "We always draw a crowd." Less pleasant are the baths, a necessity every few weeks for shorthairs, more frequently for longhaired breeds, and the subsequent blow drying, both of which start at about eight weeks.

At twelve weeks, the kittens are weaned and ready to be sold as pets or show cats. "Somehow I know the ones I'm going to keep, the way I did with Chili." I'd already met the nine-week-old red fireball careening around upstairs. "It didn't hurt that she was the runt of the litter and had to be hand fed for three weeks."

Parting with her kids, as she calls them, is less painful than we amateurs would expect. "After about twelve weeks, I'm ready to return to an adult-cat household." For the cats, the parting may be temporary: The competitive ones will likely meet again at week sixteen, when they compete at their first show.

Between the competitions and the breeding schedules, as well as her day job editing a financial-services publication, there's scant time left for other projects. Still, Iris tells me, the next night she'll be hosting an open-mike night at a local nightclub; she's trying to establish herself in one other career, as a cabaret performer. Busy as she is, says the fortysomething breeder, children were never in the picture.

"My husband was emphatically against having children, and I was ambivalent." He passed away in 1993. Things might have been different with her current boyfriend if they'd met twenty years earlier, she says. However, she rejects the idea that her cats are replacements for the children she never had.

"A woman I know who has both purebred cats and children has the best response to that," Iris tells me. "As she says, 'When a cat gives me trouble, I can sell it.'"

9

THE WILD SIDE

There's a National Geographic Society television special of which I've grown rather fond. Called *Cats: Caressing the Tiger*, it dwells on the similarities between big cats—lions and tigers and their ilk—and our house pets. The opening sequence—a fancifully intercut montage of stalking cats and prey large and small—makes its point clear from the start. When little Ginger delivers a vole, she's dreaming of the Serengeti. It's a concept worth keeping in mind.

Sara Houcke works with cats and has a better idea than many of us of our cats' wild natures. Of course, the cats Sara works with are undeniably wild—eight golden-and-white Bengal tigers—and at about five hundred pounds each only ignored at one's peril. Still, in Sara's terminology, they're her cats, and she talks with them and kisses them much like I do my Cyrus. As the tiger wrangler for Ringling Bros. and Barnum & Bailey Circus, Sara seems to regard her cats as being as responsive to her voice and her affections as I do mine.

The resemblance pretty much ends there. A tall blonde with showgirl looks, accentuated by the heavy makeup she's still wearing when we meet backstage after a matinee, Sara comes from a circus family that boasts seven generations of performers. Five have worked with animals such as horses and zebras; she has been performing since the age of two. In 1999, at the age of twenty-two, Sara became the first woman of her line since her great-great aunt to work with the big felines, tigers being the largest of the cat family.

"My dad was always saying, 'I want to work with cats,'" she recalls. He never got to, but his daughter inherited his desire. "It became my thing, and I was going, 'I want to work with cats.'" That fantasy came to fruition three years ago, when Ringling Bros. management called the Amazonian blonde to ask if she'd be interested in taking over their animal act. She'd been working with horses for the previous few years with an independent show, and llamas and camels before that, and she told the circus giants her dream. Offered the prospect of a glamorous female and wild animal act, especially in an era of increasing protests by animal-rights groups, Ringling Bros. pounced. Now "Sara and the Tigers" is a major draw for the circus's blue unit—one of two sent on the road by the international touring company.

Why tigers? "I like their looks," says the glitter-speckled star, her multinational heritage and traveling youth reflected in an accent that's part German, part Dutch, a bit English. "And lions are very . . . I mean you can go and hug and touch them, but I think they're more cold."

Tigers, Sara explains, are anything but. In the ring and out, she "chuffs" at them, making the barking sounds that translate roughly to a tiger purr. She leans her heavily mascara'd face in close to them while she chuffs, putting her head and neck in easy reach of the tigers' huge jaws and baseball-mitt-size paws, leaving herself more vulnerable to them than many other wild animal handlers would dare.

"They're like my cuddly little pets." She laughs at herself. "Which is maybe not so good, because maybe one day, you never know. I always watch out and I never forget that they are still wild animals and you never can be able to tame them. My back thought is that you always have to be careful."

My kitty is no tiger. But he is fierce, and I've seen the documentation that proves it. No matter what friends and family think when they see my twelve-pound ball of fluff, he's a fighter. That he is also a castrated, declawed (more on this later), elderly house cat doesn't matter, and I couldn't be more proud of him if he'd won a grand championship.

I always knew my cat had attitude. From that first day when he mewed up at me, I could tell he was small in stature but great in spirit, the kind of being who inspires awestruck tributes to the power of the will. But my Nietzchean little beast didn't get to show his real ferocity until he was a few years old. He must have been three or four when he and I traveled downtown for his annual shots and he finally decided he'd had enough. The trip by subway was bad; the noise and strangers commenting on him as he crouched in a swaying plastic-and-metal carrier as I held him, also huddled in a swaying, much larger plastic-and-steel carrier, was worse. By the time we got to the vet, he didn't want to be prodded. He certainly didn't want his shots. Instead, he opened his mouth and hissed. He lashed out with his clawless front paws, batting the vet's stethoscope away and began a low, deep-in-the-chest growl that made listening to his heart and lungs futile. He tried to bite.

"He's a contentious little one, isn't he?" The vet commented, trying to sound amused as she called in an assistant. The assistant arrived wearing gauntlets: thick leather gloves with arm guards that reached above her elbows. With hands nearly as long as my cat's body, she held him down so the exam could proceed. It did, under protest, but it did.

My kitty cheered right up as soon as we left the vet's office. On the ride home he looked at me without glowering, his fuzzy ears alert to catch all the curious noises of the ride. As soon as we were home he became once more a Beatrix Potter creature, all fluffy white belly and round innocent eyes. He's beaten them off, I thought. He's feeling good about himself. I didn't think much about it again for another year.

Finally, when he was about five or six, I had had enough. We had gone in again for our regular appointment: rabies, distemper, the usual. And Cyrus, as he always did, swatted at the vet, short, fast rabbit punches, as if he were boxing with leather-and-velvet gloves. He laid his ears back and bared his teeth as he jabbed at her, spit popping out with his hiss. "We have a wild one here," I remember the vet saying, the usual precursor to calling the handler. And this year when the handler came in, leather gauntlets at the ready to grab my small house cat, she asked me if I would leave the room. "It might be easier for everyone," she said, and I did. But as I stepped past the examining table I glanced down at the chart she had laid there, as she prepared to help her assistant wrestle with my pet. "FIERCE" it said on top of my cat's chart, in tall black letters highlighted with pink. "FIERCE." I felt so proud of him, outnumbered and severely outweighed. I had been part of the conspiracy to dampen his spirit, but to some extent, declawed and deballed, he was still the fighting little tom that I had first admired and then learned to love. I determined to do better by him.

Since that time we have found our current vet, Melissa, who makes house calls. Cyrus still hisses as soon as she comes in the door, a reaction Melissa attributes in part to the scent of other animals that clings from earlier appointments. He sometimes hides after she enters and sets down her black bag. But we wait for him to reappear, curious as to who the strange woman is sitting with me on the rug, and soon enough he does.

"There's my boy." She baby talks to him much like I do. "How's my boy doing?" And he'll approach her sometimes, or at least not fight when I carry him over to her. Even then, he's calmer, although he will occasionally sit there and hiss right up at her. "What a kitty!" she croons, while palpating his abdomen or listening to his heart. "He's so fierce!"

Some cats, I have since learned, don't mind going to the vet. While they may resist the intrusion of a rectal thermometer or start at an injection, they view the visit as a curiosity, an outing, and a chance to sniff very unusual odors.

Not Cyrus. Most of the time, I tell myself that this is because he is a house cat, and for the better part of his life he has lived alone with me. With no other people or animals around, Cyrus has been accustomed to a very set, sedate life, a world of finite sounds and smells. A world of routine. I tend to forget as my outside life changes, as jobs give way to other jobs and relationships grow, mutate, and die, that very little of this external activity affects my pet. My hours may vary, as I take on a new assignment, and the weekend partners might have changed in those early years more than a routine-loving cat would like, but for much of his early life—his formative years, if you will—he and I were essentially alone. It was a period of intense bonding for me, and I like to think for him as well. I was his world, my rent-controlled apartment his universe. Anything else was highly suspicious.

Increasingly, however, I have begun to worry that his reaction is not due to the appearance of a relative stranger or to his innate wild nature, but to trauma. I worry that he becomes aggressive because he fears for his life. And I blame myself for subjecting him to the treatment that he now feels he has to fight against, tooth and absent nail.

When I got my kitten, I told myself I loved his spirit. Cyrus was always an assertive kitten, a manly one even, making his desires known as loudly and obviously as he could. But in my heart I loved the soft babyness of him, much as decades ago I had loved my stuffed animals for their cuddly plush and big round eyes. For although I've never been one to coo over baby humans, baby animals have always tugged at my heart. They're so much cuter, and so much less bother.

So although I knew that at around six months I would have my cat neutered and I certainly had an intimate knowledge of male sexuality, I was still startled when I saw him cleaning himself one day and realized that among the genitalia he was licking was a small, but quite obvious, pink erection. My furry toy, my gender-neutral companion had become a sexually mature male. I had, at that point, enough trouble with men in my life. Although my cat was shy of the recommended six months, I called the vet and made an appointment.

Now, I don't really have qualms about castrating my pet. I mean, I do recall that on his return I realized I missed the sight of his tiny, fuzzy balls. But for many reasons, ranging from the political (we have way too many unwanted cats in this world) to the practical (spraying and caterwauling are not attractive indoor practices), I believe that pets should be neutered. I believe that the domestication of animals is a compromise: We shelter and feed them, as well as love them, and in return we modify their behavior and often their bodies to better fit our lives. I don't have a problem with this, in general. A neutered house cat lives a lot longer and dies a lot more peacefully than many street cats I have seen, and I think that's a fair deal. What I still have trouble putting to rest in my thoughts is the other operation I had done at the time—the declawing.

Understand, please, that there were mitigating factors. In 1984, opposition to this operation was virtually nil, at least among the cat owners and vets whom I knew. Nobody was talking about it as mutilation, nor pointing out that the name is a euphemism. (In case there are any cat lovers out there who haven't heard this yet; cats are "declawed" by having the first joint of each toe surgically removed, which is the equivalent of having your fingers chopped off at the first knuckle.) The surgery had not yet been banned in Great Britain as unnecessarily cruel. Even today, the experts are divided on it: The *Cats for Dummies* coauthors, Spadafori and Pion, are split on the surgery, particularly when it means the difference between keeping and giving up a cat. Even such a revered expert as Roger Caras has gone on record as saying that declawing is preferable to giving up a cat.

When my cat was a kitten, if this debate had begun, I never heard it. All the people I spoke with discussed the procedure as a practical, painless operation, provided that the pet owner was willing to make the commitment to keep that cat indoors, since a cat without his front claws is basically a defenseless animal. I was willing to commit to a sheltered life for my cat; I had planned on this, having already experienced the loss of one of my childhood cats to a car accident in a much more sedate suburban environment than the one Cyrus and I lived in.

And, to some extent, I had created—or at least encouraged—a

monster. Enjoying his spirit, I had not been very good at training Cyrus; by age of three or four months he scratched everything in my apartment. My furniture was old, a combination of
hand-me-downs and trash pickings, so that didn't bother me.
But when he discovered the cardboard backs of my extensive
record collection (remember, this was 1984), I became frantic.
At twelve inches high, they seemed the perfect height for him to
stretch out and grab, and grab he did, working his claws through
the glossy cardboard down to the vinyl itself. Titles and artists
disappeared, shreds of colored paper and gray board greeted me
on my return from work. T-Rex through the Wild Tchoupi-
toulas were gone, blending together in defaced anonymity.
When he discovered that, by sitting on the arm of the sofa, he
could begin on the next shelf, with the Ramones, I knew the situation was growing desperate.

I didn't give in right away. I tried the conventional remedies. I
clapped, I yelled, I tried rubbing pepper and bitter orange on the
remaining cardboard. Scratching posts imbued with catnip, covered in carpet and in corrugated cardboard went untouched.
Clipping his nails brought us both to a frenzy, and I still have the
scars to prove it. Plus even with the pointed tips trimmed off, he
clawed away. The damage those blunted claws could produce
increased almost geometrically.

I did try other options: I bought a powerful watergun and hid,
waiting, on the theory that he should believe that the blast of
water came as heaven's retribution—and therefore that even
when I was not around it could be repeated. What I got was a
wet, angry cat, a cat who vented his growing frustration with me
by tearing into that wall of vinyl. In what may be the closest I
ever get to a parental face-off with an adolescent child, I recognized defeat. I knew we were driving each other mad. I felt my

once-adorable kitten had become my enemy. The relationship was becoming untenable.

And then a friend suggested declawing. "They don't even know they no longer have them," she said to me. I read up on the procedure, learned that the hind claws are left intact so that the cat can climb to safety in case of emergency. At the time, it was considered humane and effective, and I saw that it could bring peace to my household. I called the vet back about a week before his neutering appointment. While he's under the anesthesia, I asked, can you have him declawed as well? Easiest time to do it, the woman answering the phones replied. For a small extra fee, I'd have a socially acceptable creature to share my house with again.

In all honesty, I don't think he realized that he lost his claws. His first day home, he miscalculated a jump and ended up sliding off a table more to his embarrassment than discomfort. He seemed puzzled by the newspaper that lined his litter box, mandated to prevent any irritation of his healing feet while digging. Within a few weeks the box filler had gone back to normal, and so had he. He still "scratched," marking his territory passionately and aggressively. I could watch his extended toes curl around the edge of my sofa arm, around the tops of my records, and see how he flexed and pulled. But I could observe this calmly, because no matter how he indulged his need to claw, he did no damage. Sixteen years later, he is still clawing, still marking every corner and certainly every piece of new furniture, although the CDs that came to replace those albums seem to offer less satisfaction, either because of their smaller size or their heavy plastic casing. We were at peace.

Except for his wild behavior at the vet. Over the years I would see him lashing out and although I admired his untamed spirit, I began to wonder. Was there something spurring him beside a desire to be in charge of his own body? Was he reacting more from fear than a wish for self determination? And, if so, was this because he remembered an early trauma? I thought about the operations I had submitted him to: two surgeries when he was barely six months old, a double castration—one real, one symbolic—designed for my convenience, to make my pet more docile and acceptable to my home environment. And I started to ask myself if, perhaps, there was more to the story, repercussions that I hadn't wanted to know about: Had my pet experienced more discomfort or fear than I had previously believed or been willing to admit to myself? Was there a problem, a miscalculation with the anesthesia or after treatment that meant the operation was not the painless procedure promised? Would I even have been told, considering that I clearly wanted to believe that all was easy and trauma free? I couldn't ask my cat to tell me directly, not more than his behavior already led me to believe. With so much time gone by, it was too late to ask my former vet, and I felt too guilty to inquire further.

If you look at their basic design, one thing about cats becomes clear: They are a lot closer to their wild forebears than most of the other animals we consider domestic. Cats are still effectively wild. No matter how loving they are to us, they are also efficient and well-designed carnivores, built to prowl and hunt and mate.

These days, most of us accept at least part of what I consider the domestic compromise. Most of us are aware of the benefits of neutering our cats, of truncating their sexual lives usually before they mature. Even if we eschew surgery, we're all pretty happy with the idea of training our pets out of scratching or biting as well. But even if we automatically erase these parts of their wildness, there are many other aspects of our cats' most animal nature confronting us. How we come to terms with this wild side can show us as much about ourselves as about our fierce little friends.

For every cat has a wild side, even the tamest hearth kitty. A 1987 British study (recorded in that National Geographic special) followed one small community's cats and revealed just how ferocious they are. In the village of Felmersham, a researcher, one Peter Churcher, convinced the villagers to save, and then turn over, the prey brought home by their pets. (The video has some charming footage of proud housewives handing the researcher plastic baggies of corpses, commenting with that quiet British pride: "Here's another little body for you" and "Quite a good hunter for us, isn't he?") Each of the seventy-eight village cats, Churcher found, caught on average fourteen birds or small animals a year. (The more detailed version of the study published in London's *Journal of Zoology* breaks the Felmersham cats' total prey down to 535 mammals, 297 birds, and 258 unidentified animals for the year.) From these figures, Churcher extrapolated that England's approximately five million domestic cats probably kill about seventy million fellow creatures annually, a significant slaughter of mice, voles, and sparrows.

Cyrus, unlike the village cats of Felmersham, never leaves the house. Sure, there were those two times that an inconsiderate roommate left a second-story window open and he disappeared for several hours. But he has that killer instinct, too. He "has bodies," as I like to tell friends, using prison slang culled from too many bad movies to describe the rodent corpses he laid out for me several years and two apartments ago. For as alarmed as I remember being upon learning that my apartment had mice, I was almost completely recompensed by my pride in my private hunter. "He's a little killer. Yes, he is," I would croon, my baby voice giving the lie to my words. Growing up with free-ranging cats, I knew that I didn't want all the complications of a hunting cat. I didn't want the constant parade of prey, some half dead or mutilated. But, at some level, I truly admired this element of Cyrus's animal nature.

Those first two kills startled me, it is true. But they also made me so proud. Cyrus, despite his castration, had always hit me as a very masculine cat. Call it pure projection, but something in his swagger, in his proud ruff or regal stare, gave forth a sense of confidence that always seemed leonine to me. So when he acted lionlike, displaying his kill to me—his pride—I was able easily to slip into the appropriate role. "Good boy! What an excellent fierce pouncer you are!" I even tried to avoid the baby voice, as perhaps it would be demeaning to his new status. Cyrus had bodies, after all. He was not a cat to be trifled with.

It is true that the third mouse was not as easy for me to take. That mouse did not appear as a corpse, the de facto evidence of my house cat's tiger nature. That mouse appeared, at first, as a cat toy. I was sitting on the sofa watching television, when I first noticed Cyrus playing catch. Since he was then an athletic beastie, this did not surprise me. In his youth, he would often and without provocation stalk his catnip toys, shaking them in his jaws with a spine-snapping ferocity, or kicking out with his powerful hindlegs to eviscerate this "prey." But that had been play prey. What I noticed in my peripheral vision as he tossed this "toy" was that when it landed back on my rug it moved. Of its own accord, unlike the roll of a cork or aluminum foil ball. The "toy" that my fierce companion was tossing between his forepaws over and over into the air was a living creature, a mouse, and either his play had not yet become fatal or the cushion of the rug had kept the small rodent's back from being broken, because it was trying to escape.

I panicked. Grabbing my happy cat, I tossed him into the bathroom and slammed the door. Then, quickly finding an empty spaghetti-sauce jar, I went in search of the mouse. My goal, formed in some vague humanitarian back corner of my consciousness, was to trap the smaller animal, ascertain how injured it was, and if possible, release it behind my building. Where, I guess I thought in some sentimental fashion, it would live out its life as a wild free creature of the parking lot.

Cyrus, meanwhile, was pissed. I could hear his mewing and the pounding as he battered on the bathroom door, eager to get back to his play. He knew what I did not: That mouse was capable of escape. Despite my haste, by the time I got back to the rug it was gone, and no amount of peeping under the sofa and behind the record shelves was going to turn it up again. This was a mouse that knew a lucky break when it caught one, and it was out of there.

I let Cyrus free and he immediately made an even more thorough inspection, with no better luck. I tried to pretend not to have been involved, told him that a sudden squall had blown us both into the tiny bathroom and slammed the door shut between us before I with my opposable thumbs and much greater height could release it. I don't think he bought it.

Of course, I'd been in denial about his wilder nature all along. After all, despicable as that one inconsiderate roommate may have been who had left the window open years before, that nameless housemate never pushed my dear pet out the window. Cyrus saw the opportunity to actually pursue the birds and squirrels he had so intently observed, and he went for it. That lashing tail should have clued me in earlier: My cat wanted to hunt. He is, after all, not that far removed from the giant Bengals that Sara Houcke plays with every day.

※

This is a reality that we must all come to terms with and make our peace with as we can. Buster, for example, is no tiger. But Buster, as his owner Suzi has learned, is a natural-born killer. Her "Holstein" cat, as she calls her black-and-white-spotted pet, is quite good at it, regularly bringing birds and various rodents into her apartment. "He usually shares his prey," says the Korean-American musician, sounding half proud and half, I suspect, resigned. "He likes to bring me the heads."

Her big, floppy Buster wasn't always so ferocious. As a tiny abandoned kitten brought into her boyfriend's workplace, she'd had to dropper feed him. Too young to have learned the basics, he didn't even know how to use the litter box until Suzi trained him herself—"by getting in there and digging around."

Because she then lived in a wooded area, she thought the young cat should experience nature. At first, Buster wanted nothing to do with the great outdoors.

"He was terrified." She remembers the kitten refusing to leave her boyfriend's lap. "He put one paw out and pulled it back. He went in concentric circles, walked around, and came back." Soon, however, he was exploring and asking to go out, and she can only assume he watched other cats and learned to kill from them. "Once he was out and about, he was out and about," she says. "His basic nature is very aggressive."

For Suzi, the learning curve has been a tad steeper. "The first time he brought home prey, it was a bird. A sparrow. No head, just the body. There it was on the doorstep with him. He was very proud of himself. I was absolutely horrified. I ran around shrieking but my boyfriend said, 'No, no, no! This is the biggest sign of love a cat can give. We have to praise him.'

"So we stroked him and we cuddled him and praised him." The positive reinforcement (or something more basic) had an effect Suzi hadn't anticipated: more prey. "The first time he brought me a mouse it was horrible. I couldn't touch it for three days," she sighs. "I got used to it."

The seagull was another turning point. "The gull was bigger than Buster, but he got it. He took it down. There were feathers everywhere, white feathers floating down the street.

"Then the real clincher was the bird that was still alive." Buster seemed to have his own idea of food prep. When Suzi, unaware, opened the door, he'd brought the small brown bird into the kitchen and put it down by his dish. Immediately upon its release, the wounded bird tried to escape. Fluttering frantically, it headed down the hall and Buster went after it, cornering the bleeding animal in Suzi's bathroom.

"There were feathers and blood and a panicked bird and a cat hunting the bird." In the small apartment bathroom, nature took its course. "It was *Wild Kingdom* in my bathroom," Suzi recalls. "And I had to clean up all the gore."

Still with her philosophical bent, the musician had taken her friend's advice to heart. Bringing home prey was what a good cat did. Since she had chosen to cohabit with a carnivore, she would have to come to terms with this. She soon had an opportunity.

"The middle of the night, I heard the *ch-ch-ch-ch* of an animal. Buster got up and parked himself by the stove, and I got up and decided to watch. And that was the night the mouse we'd known was in there finally emerged from the stove. As I watched, Buster pounced on it and took it into the corner and was playing with it. He let it go and then he brought it back. He let it go and brought it back again. Then he broke its leg. Then he dealt the death blow and systematically ate it, from its head down to the toes.

"This was the same cat that would crawl into bed with me ten minutes later. *Prr-rr-rr-rr*," she imitates the deep, rich purr of a contented feline. "I had to come to terms with this, with his violence and his sheer love of torture," says Suzi. This, she reasoned, was a large part of who Buster is: "He kills and tortures with no need for the food. He gets Iams and Whiskas and Pounce treats every day of his life, and he has no need to do this. It's his programming. It's just as much a part of his nature as the cute and cuddly and sweet."

I think about our lives, about Suzi, who splits her time between her college day job, her yoga, and her nights playing piano and accordion, and I wonder how much of her experience with Buster translates to the wider world. She and I talk about our own capacity for violence, our own propensity toward rage despite all the civilizing influences of our educations, our jobs, and the arts we've both committed to. Her time with Buster, she begins to explain, has actually brought her closer to the higher consciousness she seeks.

"I think that it makes me much more aware of, and understanding of, anger and frustration and violence," she begins. "It makes me accept more that this is in every human being, to accept this part of ourselves, and to choose our behavior intelligently."

The word *samadhi*—a Buddhist concept referring to a state of consciousness in which all is accepted and understood, a step toward higher meditation—comes up. "I've learned that truly letting go and relaxing and accepting and being—any of us can do that." Buster, both friendly and terrifyingly fierce, serves as a perfect example. "With cats, one minute they're sinuous bone and muscle and the next moment they're just a lump of fur. That's why they are so peaceful.

"A cat is very Zen. It shows you a picture, a metaphor through which to understand life," Suzi concludes. "And we're devoted to each other, we're loyal to each other. It's a weird partnership. He trained me as I trained him. We balance each other."

We each must find such balance, and what works for one pairing doesn't necessarily fit another. Take the question of indoors or out, for example. There's no argument about the facts: Indoor cats, as all the experts agree, live healthier and longer, on average twice as long. They are prone to fewer diseases, fewer fights and bites, and are less likely to be hit by cars or be poisoned by accident or malice. But for many of us, these are not the only factors. The question of whether to let our cats out calls into play everything we feel about them as individuals and as domesticated animals, and how we picture ourselves as caretakers, pet owners, or considerate fellow creatures.

Most of us have opted to neuter our pets and public opinion has turned against declawing. The question of whether we, the cat lovers of the world, would opt for a genetically modified hypoallergenic cat is probably years off, although one biotechnology firm, Transgenic Pets of Syracuse, New York, is looking into cloning what would essentially be a danderless cat. For many of us, however, the issue of whether to let a cat go out or keep it in is very current and much more difficult, bringing up questions that resonate to the heart of the relationship.

"I let my cat Lunar go out. It started accidentally," reports Carrie, a San Francisco–based Web site editor. "I lived in a first-floor flat with three guys. The back door opened up into our fenced-in backyard, and the door was always being left open and I got sick of retrieving the cat. He has very poor eyesight and has traditionally been pretty timid, so I didn't worry too much about him, plus all of a sudden there was no litter box to clean.

"Recently Luney was sick, pooing blood and throwing up, and it was then that I felt terribly guilty about letting him go outside. I was certain he'd been poisoned by someone's garden chemicals or something. The vet advised keeping him in for a week, which I did, but he's now back to his indoor/outdoor schedule and seems fine. How do I ameliorate the guilt? I only let him out when I'm at home, and he stays out only for a short time, usually. I know he could still come into contact with harmful substances in a short jaunt from home, but when he stays inside, I almost feel like I'm keeping him imprisoned. I like the idea that he decides for himself when to come in and when to go out. I keep his vaccines up to date, and he gets some freedom of choice."

"My three cats are strictly indoors—and I have absolutely no guilt about it," says Dee, who works with the feral cats who have bred into huge colonies in her home base of Little Rock. "I believe that when we take an animal and domesticate it, we have a moral obligation to keep it safe from harm. Although I live in a fairly rural area, any animal I had that went outside would have to contend with traffic, dogs, parasites, and a neighbor I have who hates cats, too. Cat owners in my neighborhood are pretty much convinced that this guy was the one who spiked tunafish with antifreeze in an attempt to get rid of a sizable feral cat colony." (Antifreeze tastes sweet, but is lethal to cats.)

"If I had lots of money, I would consider enclosing my deck with screens to let them out in a controlled environment," Dee concludes. "But the budget rules, and the cats stay indoors."

What is coming into conflict is our desire to keep our cats safe and our equally intense hunger to make our pets happy. Because as any cat lover will agree, the cat is the natural enemy of the closed door. Even within a house, it is antithetical to a cat to have a portal closed off. We love them, and they want out. It is a difficult call.

This is, in large part, why Lynne's cat Morticio has only six lives left. Morticio is what T. S. Eliot would call a jellicle, a small, neat black-and-white tuxedo cat, who has seen more than his two and a half years would seem to merit. Originally named Morticia, until a visit to the vet set Lynne straight, he's now an altered gentle cat, one who only occasionally brings home a bird or mouse. But Morticio likes to go out, to prowl through the bushes and small woods of Lynne's suburb, even if he hasn't had much success as a hunter. And despite Morticio's three brushes with death in not as many years, Lynne lets him.

The first mishap was probably due to a car. Lynne never saw the accident that left her small cat to limp up her driveway with a bloody nose when she returned from work one evening.

But Morticio displayed some discomfort and he was dragging one leg, so although he ate and slept normally that night Lynne brought him into the animal hospital the next morning. X rays turned up a broken jaw, which the vet wired, and several broken teeth, which had to be removed.

The X rays revealed more serious damage as well: a fractured pelvis was causing his "funny walk" and that would take longer to mend. While his bones healed, Lynne tried in vain to keep Morticio quiet, putting up barriers to restrain him from jumping and reinjuring his pelvis. But by the time she was ready to abandon the battle of wits, Morticio had healed. And he waited, once more, by the back door after breakfast to be let out on his daily rounds.

"Letting him out after that was hard," recalls Lynne. "I don't live that far from Route 9," a major thoroughfare with four fast-moving lanes that's busy most of the day. "I said to myself, maybe his experience has taught him to be wary of cars," she remembers. And she let him commence his roaming. A few months later, Morticio stopped eating, ill with what the vet could only call a fever of unknown origin. Although she can't tell for sure if he picked up this particular bug in his rambles through the neighborhood, in all likelihood he did. As well as the increased risk of accidents, cats who prowl outside the house are subject to a variety of diseases, including the feline equivalents of leukemia and AIDS. Six days into his illness, Morticio was an extremely sick cat. Although intravenous sustenance kept him alive, the antibiotics that the vet was also pumping into his system didn't seem to be working. It was time, Lynne's vet told her, to think of putting Morticio to sleep.

She asked for the night to think over her decision. When she called in the morning her mind was made up. Deeply saddened though she was, Lynne agreed that it was time. This was not the life her happy, active cat had come to love. She made the call. But the vet who answered had good news. Morticio was eating. He was weak, but he was responsive. The vet was cautiously optimistic. In a few days, his black-and-white fur was once more glossy, his eyes bright. Morticio was his old self again.

The round-eyed kitty's third brush with death was the one that taught Lynne most what she was risking. As soon as he was healthy enough, Morticio resumed his practice of waiting by the door, ready to go out in the mornings when Lynne left for work. One night, however, he was not waiting on the outside of that door for her upon her return. Nor, when she called, did she see his sleek almond-shaped form racing up her drive. Morticio was gone.

She didn't worry for a day or two, but then the images began to form. He had been hit by a car, and not so lightly this time. He had become trapped in someone's truck or car trunk, a basement or garage, and was unable to escape. Around this time, someone pointed out to her that coyotes had begun to invade the suburbs around her own, and the idea that her darling pet had become prey to a larger carnivore took shape.

Throughout these horrible fantasies, Lynne searched for Morticio. She posted fliers and called local shelters in the hope that he had shed his collar, but been picked up as a lost pet. Eventually, she began talking to friends about grief, of the resignation that was growing in her to mourn the cat she called "my little source of unconditional love," comforting herself with the fantasy that someone had taken him in, taken him for their own dear pet. After two weeks, it seemed unlikely she would see the glossy tuxedo cat again.

A month went by, and Lynne stopped looking. But one evening, as she pulled into her driveway she saw a small dark shape. It was a cat, and although it was thin and it was dirty, it looked suspiciously like her lost pet. Lynne thought she was hallucinating but knowing better than to question good fortune she let the starving feline in and watched him devour two cans of food before promptly curling up on her pet's favorite chair and falling asleep. Morticio had returned.

For a few days after that, there would be no thought of letting him back out. But a few weeks later, he resumed his morning watch by the door, and Lynne faced the difficult decision.

"We had that talk," she says. "I said, 'I can tell you aren't made to be an indoors cat. But you have to make some compromises. You have to wear your collar. And you have to come back at night.' "

Whether Morticio agreed with these stipulations—some might ask whether he even understood the nature of the conversation—Lynne was satisfied.

"I understand the dilemma," she says. "Do I keep him an indoors cat and let myself be happy that he's protected, or do I let him be what he wants to be, an indoors-outdoors cat? I thought, if it were me I'd want to go out. For me, it was identifying what I would choose myself."

For a growing number of unfortunate felines, outdoors is not an option, it's a life sentence. Although no solid numbers exist for the feral cat population, there are clearly hundreds of thousands, if not millions, of abandoned pets and their offspring. These numbers are no exaggeration; simple cat math shows the possibilities. According to the National Humane Education Society, one unspayed female and one intact male can produce two litters a year. With a low estimated survival rate of 2.8 kittens per litter that can mean approximately twelve new cats in the first year. (Don't forget, each litter will be breeding before its first birthday.) Computing all the breeding possibilities, this family can grow to 68 cats in two years, 367 cats in five years, and 2,107 cats in eight years. The numbers don't stop, topping 2 million cats in less than eight years.

These are not footloose and fancy-free animals. Descendants of housecats, they are smaller and less able to care for themselves than their wild ancestors, and they are easy prey for coyotes and wolves, not to mention dogs or the more vicious of our own kind. Their coats do not protect them from snow or frost or heavy rains. Once sickened or weakened by hunger or by fighting, even among themselves, these cats are even more vulnerable to predators, to illness, and to the violence, careless or intentional, of humans.

These cats do not enjoy proud lives. Many turn up in shelters mutilated from fights or accidents, and most end up dying young of disease or the elements, mauled or eaten by predators. A lucky few, like Isis and Luna, end up with second chances: "When we moved into the house, I saw all these cats roaming around. I kept hearing them meow," says Barb. January in Iowa is not kind weather, and she was worried. "I thought, 'I have extra food, I'll go out and feed them.' It became a ritual." She doesn't know what happened to the scarred old tom she'd seen with the small pride, but she soon captured the two queens and brought them into her covered porch. Two years later, they're both still skittish, but have more or less settled in with Barb, her boyfriend, and the two house cats with which the couple had begun. "I thought, I would want someone to take in my cats if they were lost," says Barb. "I've always been an animal person."

To help combat the common tragedy of feral cats and to put such caring instincts to use on a larger scale, a growing number of feral cat "rescue" programs have begun around the country. Nonprofit groups like Alley Cat Allies of Washington, D.C., Town Cats of Maryland, and Friends of Plymouth Pound in Massachusetts work both to reduce the number of such animals and their suffering. Sometimes that means trapping, neutering, and releasing feral cats, with the aim of keeping the populations stable and reducing disease; often these groups euthanize fatally ill or dying cats. At other times, volunteers shelter and attempt to socialize the usually fearful ferals, with mixed results.

These cats, unlike stray or abandoned pets, are not accustomed to human company. Raised with little or no contact with people, they scatter and hide at our approach, as they did the afternoon I visited Gayle, the powerhouse brunette behind the Friends of Plymouth Pound. Upstairs, in her suburban ranch, I'd already met Ringo and Champ, her pet cats, and heard of Blossom and Steve, her adopted semiferals (who made themselves scarce throughout my visit). And as we descended the stairs into her basement—one of three shelters the Friends operate—the scratch of frantic scrambling that greeted me made me anticipate a zoo. I could smell cat urine, despite Gayle's daily cleaning. But I saw nothing beyond cat boxes and blankets, makeshift cat beds and large sacks of litter and dry food.

"You've got to look closely," said Gayle, leading me over to a partially finished wall. There, above me, hung a tail, plumed out and luxurious. Two blue eyes glared from the space between wall and ceiling and disappeared, as their owner retreated farther into the unconstructed space. Another pair took their place, and suddenly I was aware of feline faces all along the open structure, of movement in the nooks and crannies of the large basement. These eyes, wary and alert, followed us as we walked into a cage area, where a few old timers who had tested positive for feline leukemia or feline immunodeficiency disease were sheltered, and they followed us back as Gayle bent to haul a bag of litter, in preparation for her daily duties.

"Some of them will find homes," she said of the thirty-seven cats then sheltered in the two basement rooms, speaking with hope I certainly couldn't have mustered. Sure enough, in the months that followed, some became accustomed to the sound of her voice, to the presence of other Plymouth volunteers, and have been placed as pets. But even as we made the rounds that afternoon, meeting the inhabitants of the cages—stopping to chat with battered old Clyde, a longhaired gray who was missing an ear, or the tiger-striped Randy—Gayle didn't seem overly worried. Nor did she seem bothered by the fear and hissing that greeted her approach. Like her forty volunteers, primarily women, of course, Gayle is motivated by a passion somewhat different from that of the average pet owner. They are looking to help otherwise friendless animals rather than bond with these cats as pets. "Most of them tell me that they volunteer because they love the cats," she says. "It's like therapy and they enjoy spending time with them, and they feel good knowing they have saved a life."

A similar emotion compels those women, and again, it is primarily women, who do the active rescue work of trapping. Gina and Janice have both been involved with Town Cats in Ocean City, Maryland, for several years, and have focused their efforts on neutering as many of the feral cats as they can. "It's a farm mentality out here," explains Gina, a graphic designer by trade. "Animals are considered disposable." She's talking about the colonies they find, where generations of cats have inbred and infected each other with various diseases after being abandoned by the people who once loved them.

Janice, the woman who originally feared cats, helps out trapping the terrified ferals. Recently Town Cats has begun to work with a large colony at an abandoned racetrack. Cats have been dumped here for years, she explains, and various homeless people—squatters—kept many as half-socialized pets. Recently the problem has become exacerbated by new owners who have taken over the track, evicting the people and threatening to destroy all the resident cats. Town Cats is doing what it can, and Janice gets out there once a week. Some of the cats, she says, can be socialized, and the group works with stores like PetSmart that let them offer such rescued cats up for adoption. Some get their shots and their operations and are released, a fortunate few make it into a temporary shelter that the group has just set up. Some are not so lucky.

"Our colony right now has an outbreak of feline panleukopenia," she reports. Pets are commonly vaccinated against this virus, also known as distemper, which spreads quickly and is usually fatal. "We've found three dead cats at our last visit, and it's just shattered us," she says. Some of the infected include the sixty-plus cats that one of the squatters—a woman, of course—had taken in. "We got about half of them to the vet. Half of them were very tame, and we're getting them adopted. The other half are not so tame."

The work is a real labor of love, and not always repaid in kind. "We wear leather gloves and long-sleeved sweatshirts. We've all gotten ringworm. We're used to being scratched," says Janice. Sometimes, however, there is a payoff. "We've gotten a lot of feral cats who've gotten tame because we've given them a lot of love."

"We can't save 'em all, certainly not," adds Gina. "But at least you make a difference in certain communities."

All of us who love cats have probably at some point fantasized about working with them. We picture ourselves coming in to change litter boxes at animal hospitals, or to play with the lonely older cats at the various no-kill shelters that seem so humane and friendly. But as Janice and Gina and their sisters across the country illustrate, doing the real work of helping cats can be more difficult than we'd imagined. For Monique, it comes close to breaking her heart.

Luckily, Monique has her cat Minster to help her relax. "She's my goddess," the dark, intense woman tells me without irony. "The moment I put my hand on her she sucks the stress out of me. I feel the tension flowing out." Although the plump gray-and-orange calico has been a bit put out by my arrival at the end of the workday, she comes forward to greet me, daintily sniffing my outstretched fingers, white nose taking in the smell of ink and the outdoors and of my Cyrus. "I have a fascination with witchcraft. I don't know much about paganism," continues Monique, sipping her after-work coffee. "But I wonder: If people knew how much I revere my cat, would they put me in that category?"

Monique is a musician, although she doesn't yet make a living from the strong rhythmic compositions she creates. Her large, somewhat run-down apartment is filled with instruments and with her paintings, composed—as is her wardrobe—with lots of black and stark shapes. Perhaps it was inevitable that any commitment she'd make would be a full-throttle one. Monique doesn't hold much back. But until Minster entered her life, she never intended such an intense relationship with a cat.

"I wasn't always sold on cats," she explains. "I'd been brought up to think that the real companion is a dog." Although she acquired her first cat in the second grade, her family also had dogs, huskies and the like, which the young girl had always considered the more important family pets. Minster came to her through a roommate, who adopted the cat from a shelter and then moved on to a no-pet apartment. The round calico, Monique says, always preferred her to the departing roommate anyway. "And I absolutely adore her." That was five years ago.

Since then, Monique has supplemented her music with a variety of jobs, most recently at a regional nonprofit animal shelter. The job, as well as her growing love for Minster, has changed her view on what makes a proper pet. "Now that I work in a shelter," she says, "I realize that dogs are more of a luxury animal. They require more attention, more pampering. You have to have a job that you can take off from a few times a day, or you have to be able to pay someone to walk them. Cats are very different animals; they're for very different people.

"I didn't really see the beauty of cats until I started to live with one. Now I feel super in-tune with cats. You could really categorize me with the Egyptians: I think cats spiritually are on a much higher level than other animals. Cats know things that humans cannot comprehend."

Monique has several examples readily at hand. Minster is more than a pet, she's a friend, a "sister," the woman sipping coffee explains, a fellow creature who understands the stress currently coursing through Monique's life. For starters, there's the eviction. Although Monique's landlord is giving her plenty of time, the big old house she lives in is being renovated and sold. The dark-haired musician with the facial piercings wants to move to New York, where many of her friends live and where she could more wholeheartedly pursue her music. However, her boyfriend Jim has strong ties to the Boston area.

"It's put a strain on me and Jim," she says, explaining how, if the argument continues into the bedroom, Minster will insert herself between the bickering couple, pushing up against one and then the other, demanding to be petted, defusing the situation. "Every time we have an argument or are sounding more frustrated, Minster knows from the beginning of the discussion what it's going to become. She'll come in and sit perfectly still. But if my voice starts going up, she'll crouch down, her eyes half closed. She's talking to me. I would swear sometimes when I'm upset that she says to me, 'Monique, don't be so upset. We've been through some hard times. This isn't any harder.'

"It's funny, after all we've been through. I think she's the strongest one of the three of us. They endure, you know?"

Then there is Monique's job.

"Some of the calls we get, you can't believe," she tells me. "People call to say they found a kitten in a trash can. People call to say, 'There are cats in my yard. Get them out of here.' Every couple of days I get that anonymous call, someone yelling 'murderer.' "

One of Monique's duties—along with cleaning the approximately 250 cages, grooming, and giving innoculations—is performing euthanasia. Roughly 70 percent of the three to four million cats who enter shelters each year are euthanized, according to the American Society for the Prevention of Cruelty to Animals. For Monique, that means during "kitten season," the period between April and September when free-ranging cats do most of their breeding, she has to help kill as many as twenty to thirty cats each day. She and her colleagues, who are all certified in humane euthanasia, use a commercial product called Fatal Plus, which essentially gives the cat an overdose of phenobarbital. The cat literally goes to sleep. Not that this makes it easier for Monique.

"I've come so close to quitting this job so many times. It's so hard," she says. "Every time I euthanize a cat it's very difficult."

As long as people are irresponsible about their animals, she explains, there is no alternative. "Wherever there is a no-kill shelter, there's a regular shelter nearby." She sounds resigned. "We tell people when they surrender their cats that our age limit is eight for adoptions." She and her colleagues often bend the rules, she explains, fudging birth dates when a cat seems like it might get a second chance with a new home. However, if the cat is ill or aggressive when it is evaluated, it gets euthanized. "We tell people that. We tell people that coming to a shelter is very stressful for a cat, but they go, 'Oh, my cat is so friendly, she'll get adopted.' Then they call the next day, and I have to tell them that their cat was euthanized. That their cat bit an attendant or tried to scratch the vet, and we had to euthanize her."

The job, she explains, is a "love-hate thing." Although Monique had worked in a shelter as a teenager, she never before had to deal with euthanasia. As a teenage volunteer, she'd been too young. And as a child, she had been sheltered from the final reality. "I'd had pets put to sleep before, but I'd never seen them put to sleep. It was like, I'd start crying. I'd kiss the animal good-bye, and Mom or Dad would take her away."

Now living in a city heavily populated by students and transients, she sees hundreds of cats surrendered because of housing problems and lifestyle changes: new landlords, allergic roommates, and owners who simply no longer want the hassle.

She recalls the day she and her co-workers were trained to perform euthanasia. The session began with a series of videos that showed how animals could be restrained, that showed the effects of the various poisons.

"When we were all done watching the videos, we all went down to 'Lethal,'" the room where the euthanasia is performed, she explains. "I thought, this is awful. I think certain people and certain animals can smell death. We saw the Fatal Plus, and it was just an awful feeling.

"We're trained to tranquilize them first," she explains, talking about the ketamine, which has also gained a reputation as an illicit party drug for humans, who have nicknamed it "Special K." "That was the worst part. Some of the animals have a reaction to it. It's not quick enough for me.

"When we were all done being trained we were all wiping our eyes," she remembers. "I remember one woman saying, 'I can't do this. I just can't do this.'"

She pauses. It's been a long day. "I think about quitting all the time," she says. "I remember what the vet teaching us told me that day: 'You want to get very good at this, because you want it to be quick and painless. You want to be the best you can be. But never get used to it.' "

10

LETTING GO

AUGUST

I love my kitty. In my mind, he's still my kitty, the tiny bundle of fur that fit into the palm of my hand and stole my heart, sixteen and a half years ago. In those days he was as light as a puffball, all his size filled out by long gray fur that smelled like talcum powder, and those ears, big as a bat's, that nearly tripled the size of that small determined face.

These days, my dear kitty, my Cyrus T. Cat, is almost weightless again. Long gone are the days when our vet cautioned me against overfeeding. Years past are the lectures on the health problems of overweight cats, or the friends who commented—unkindly, I thought, since I too have had my struggles with weight—that Cyrus was more portly than proper. When my kitty hit his thirteenth birthday, he began to lose weight. On his fourteenth, after tests for thyroid turned up normal, we accepted his lighter stature as part of the muscle loss of aging. A year later, we had his thyroid tested again, and then other tests, which did not come back so well. And for the past year and a half, my husband and I have struggled to digest the knowledge that our Cyrus's kidneys are slowly failing, and that this, as well as some possible intestinal disease, has pared down our once solid sixteen-pounder to now weigh in at half that.

This makes my husband, who has known and, I think, loved Cyrus for half his life, very sad. To me, who raised this little creature, who nurtured the sickly runt of the litter into a strong, beautiful, and, I believe, happy cat, it is nearly incomprehensible. I feel so guilty now, for faults real and imagined; for serving him the prescription food that he does not enjoy as much as his old supermarket cans; for leaving to work; for leaving on our increasingly brief vacations, knowing that—despite the cat-sitting we arrange, the friends who promise to linger for hours and pet and converse with my darling—he will miss us. I worry that he will miss me, and that he is failing. I tell myself that it is not my fault that he is failing, but this is hard to accept.

He has been everything to me at times. And even if I now have a more full life than I did when he first came into it, even if I am now happily married and surrounded by good and dear friends, he is still my kitty.

These days, my kitty seems more affectionate than ever. Although he always had the habit of kneading me, his ears pitched forward in an attitude of concentration that always made me smile, about two years ago he began to do so nightly in preparation for settling in the crook of my arm, where he would sleep for hours, sometimes through till morning. He has become more willing to be held these past few years, and sometimes these days even climbs onto my lap when I put my feet up for a night of television or reading. He has become jealous of my laptop computer, invariably pawing at me in a seeking way when I rest this foreign plastic beast on my legs instead of him.

I realize that this behavior may be prompted as much by a desire for comfort as for affection, that as he ages he may have grown to appreciate the warmth of a human body as well as its owner's attentions. And I've come to accept that he no longer always smells like talcum powder. In fact, his litter-box training, which always tended to lapse in times of emotional upset—when I was away on vacation, for example, or the one time a neighbor cat wandered in through an open door—has declined. He's still a clean cat: he may shit on the sofa occasionally, but he always washes himself afterward. He also seems more flatulent than in years past, and his grooming of his long silky hair has declined to the point where we must remove the occasional felted dreadlock, or risk his still sharp and plentiful teeth while trying to comb them out.

We have been on an adventure. Although it has taken turns I could not have predicted and must, I tell myself, be nearing its end, I do not in any way regret my choice, which launched our voyage together. I tell myself I have given my pet a good life, a full life, as healthy and happy as any domesticated animal can expect. I have loved my little Cyrus. He has outpaced me in aging, but we have grown up together. He has taught me about the mysterious bond between women and cats, and as he sits now at the foot of the bed, nose tucked neatly into tail tip and purring, I feel a communion that perhaps only other cat lovers can understand. He is my kitty, my Cyrus, my cat. And I am his human, his partner, for however long fate has us linked.

Diane, whose senior cat, Rossi, is nineteen years old, is facing some of the same issues: fear of loss, the complications of illness. Rossi's still a big, rangy cat, although his gray-striped back and long white legs are lean to the point of emaciation and his thick, short fur is scruffier than in his youth. He passes by us as we set-tle onto the sofa, walking stiffly into the kitchen for another drink of water while Diane and I talk.

"I started noticing a big difference in him about a year ago," says Diane, a comfortably built woman with a tendency to laugh at herself. "He began to lose a lot of weight. I think he has some hearing difficulties. Sometimes I think his age has given him the ability to ignore what he doesn't want to hear." I tell her about an elderly relative who, I believe, uses her slight deafness in such a way, and she chuckles. "Exactly! He picks and chooses what he wants to hear."

Her other cat, a huge longhair named Robby, comes in to head-butt me, pushing his thickly furred head against my hand. When I reach for him, expecting the plush softness of an over-weight cat, I find instead solid muscle, maybe twenty pounds under all that fur. This is more muscle than I've ever felt in a cat, and when he wriggles in my startled grasp, I drop him. Non-plussed, he walks away with the peculiar high-rumped walk of a Manx, and Diane relates his history.

In his own way, Robby's life has been disrupted by aging. Robby had lived with Diane's mother until a few years ago. She had to give him up when she moved into an assisted-living cen-ter, and Diane and her husband took him in. Still, having him here, says Diane, has been a comfort. "For everyone but Rossi!" She laughs again, and then corrects herself, as we both acknowl-edge the physical differences between her two pets.

"They get along. I don't think Rossi was thrilled when he moved in, but they'd stayed together in the past when we'd gone on vacation. They knew each other. Rossi was still pretty feisty then. He ruled: All he had to do was raise a paw and Robby would back off. Now it doesn't work that way. I'll be in bed in the morning and Robby will come in and lie next to me and purr and purr and purr. And Rossi will come in. It's hard for him to get into the bed now, but he'll claw his way up. And he'll get very angry at finding Robby there, and he'll whack him or bite him on the ear. And then Robby will chase him off the bed. Rossi doesn't realize yet that he's quite geriatric. And Robby will defer to him in some things, like if I put the food down and it's particularly interesting, he'll back off and let Rossi eat. But the power base is shifting."

The lean older cat joins us in the living room, then leaves again. I suspect he's returned to the oversize water bowl Diane has left out for him. We talk about hydrating cats subcutaneously, about watching them waste away and grow slow and unstable.

"It's very sad when they start to fade." Diane's voice has gone soft. "Obviously you love them and you don't want them to go away, and you don't want them to suffer. And it brings up all kinds of questions of mortality.

"I don't know, it's been . . ." She pauses, and I can't tell if she's searching for the right word or if she is holding back tears. "He used to be kind of a tough cat, a big tough cat. And I've had to get used to treating him in a different way. I mean, I never used to kick him around, but I'm being extra gentle with him.

"The vet says now, 'Just keep him eating. Just keep him eating at this point.' So I do. He loves shrimp; I feed him shrimp. I know the inevitable is coming. He surprised me actually. There was a period when he went into a steep decline, and then he leveled off. That was about a year ago, when his kidney and thyroid conditions seemed to get worse. He had been losing weight and then, I thought, 'Oh god, I hope he doesn't have cancer, too.' But it was just this, and the medication seems to help. A year ago, I wouldn't have said he'd be around for another year, but he is.

"The vet gave me a prescription to get filled, and it was an enormous bottle of pills. I only give him a half a pill a day, but he's used almost all of them. Haven't you, you devil?" The old cat walks up to his woman and jumps to her lap, a bit stiff, but he makes it.

OCTOBER

I dream about losing Cyrus. I dream of him dying, and of his death, in much the same way I dreamed of my father's death before it happened. It is as if all the daytime helplessness, encapsulated in panic, has found a way to burst open at night, into my sleep, and flood me with the images I freeze out during the day.

I tell myself the dreams are different. I do not dream anything prophetic, I tell myself, trying to reassure myself in the cold sweat of waking. I had, in fact, foreseen my father's death before he told me of its imminence. Not that I saw it directly, but I saw *him* sitting, alone, in a stadium, after the crowds departed, and I felt him gripped by an enormous final sadness. In retrospect, after he told me of the cancer that had by then metastasized through his bones, I believed that what I had sensed earlier, before his news, was his emotional state. That, unable or unwilling to interpret what I had sensed in my waking hours, I had let myself visualize this final loneliness in my sleep.

I do not dream of Cyrus in exactly that way, and therefore I reassure myself that despite our connection, I am not being clairvoyant.

The first dream, or at least the first I remember, had some of the same emotional flavor as my dreams of my father, the same sadness and—for me—the same guilt. In the first dream, I was directly to blame. We had been staying in some bucolic woodland cabin, something on a hillside, with trees and deer. And in the morning, Cyrus and I had both stepped outside, and I had left him there, a lifelong house cat, now elderly. I had told him that I would be back within an hour, reassuring him as I often do now and seeing his wide-eyed adorable face look up at my words of return. And I had left him. Outside.

Of course, hours later in dreamtime, I return, and he is nowhere to be seen. He is not, as I assume I had imagined in the dream's early scenes, standing on the spot where I last saw him, slim body in profile, round little face turned up to mine. And he does not answer to my call.

What I do notice, which of course I had not before, are the number of other animals about, predatory animals like dogs, and larger cats, and even bears. I call and call and berate myself with each repetition of his name. How could I have been so stupid? How could I have been so blind? After all my years of vigilance, to let him out! Then I go behind the cabin, where the hillside slopes upward in mossy stillness. It's peaceful here; there are no threatening animals here. Could he have gone this way? I am overcome by hope, even though I still see no sign of him. I know that the elements, that nature itself will be against him—thin, frail by nature's standards, in the cold outdoors—but I see that green soft wilderness stretching upward and my panic eases a bit. I guess that is the closest to heaven I can picture. But when I woke on that image and found my warm and breathing pet lying next to me, I gently held him, willing him not to notice my attentions and jump off the bed as is his wont. I went back to sleep with him lying beside me, comforting me.

The last dream was more realistic, perhaps, although it still involved an element of guilt, of my not fulfilling the careful owner's contract. In this dream, once again, I had let Cyrus out of the house. I had let him out, exposed, to strange territory and other animals. The scene opens and he is sitting by the road in a rural setting, the tall dry grass half hiding him. He sits, feet tucked under at his most relaxed position. We are waiting to start a New Year's party, a costume party, even though the air is warm and the sun is baking down on the yellow-brown grass that reaches above my knees. And somehow I know a vet is coming, perhaps as an invited guest.

That's who brings the trouble in this dream, although the fact of Cyrus's location comes back to haunt me, especially as the vet tells me how sick my cat is. "His kidneys have ceased to function at all," this dream vet tells me. "Didn't your vet warn you that he was on his last reserves?" he asks. No, I respond at first. Then I remember, with guilt, that in fact she had, but I had not wanted to do another blood level test at that moment, since we were dealing with his intestinal woes and he seemed to be functioning at more or less the same level as he had at her last visit. (A decision I had actually made after talking to Melissa a few weeks before.) "We were going to test his levels again in the spring." I am taken back by the suddenness of it all. Wouldn't there be some twilight period? I wonder. Wasn't there supposed to be some period where his kidneys had all but failed, but he could live, and for a while enjoy his prolonged life through the intervention of subcutaneous hydration? I had been preparing to accept this step in the future, in the next summer perhaps, when the heat began to contribute to his dehydration. Not now, in this preternaturally warm winter. Was I to have no warning?

"But he has been so lively," I tell the dream vet. "He has been gaining weight back. He has been playful." I tell the vet of his athletic prowess, including his newfound vice of jumping to the countertops at night, the result probably of his being confined to the back of the house due to occasional incontinence, and to boredom. "It's a high jump," I tell the vet. "I never hear him until he knocks something over, a cereal box or a pot balanced on the dish rack."

"That is all illusion. He has no kidney function left," the

dream vet responds, and I wonder if Melissa, our waking vet, has been trying to tell me this too. I think of Cyrus sitting in his kitchen window, eyeing birds and squirrels alike with deadly intent and a hunter's lashing tail. I think of his voracious appetite, at least now that I have broken his diet of modified, kidney-friendly food on the premise that how much he ate was, at this point, as important as what he ate. I think of how responsive he is, his morning mews and demands for pets. To no avail.

But the dream vet gives me an out, buys me some time. "He is drinking so much and he is so smart that he has circumvented the need for his kidneys' filtering function," this vet tells me. "He is filtering himself, for now. You must be very careful to always have fresh, very clean water available for him. You are living on borrowed time with him."

Of course, I think of the slightly scummy water dish then, changed that morning but sullied by his paw, which he uses to break the water's surface before drinking, and by the bits of food that increasingly these days cling to his face. I race to the house to change his dish, and race back to the roadside to retrieve my cat, still soaking up the sun in the tall grasses. I am terrified. This is much too soon. That once again I have let my pet down with less than ideal care eats at me, as does my oh-so impending loss. I should not have mixed quite so much Fancy Feast in with the Modified Care prescription diet. I should have changed the water just one more time before bed. I should not have looked the other way, not have panicked, when his weight first started to drop.

I wake again to find my cat in his usual place beside me on the bed. I find that although he did not join us when we first retired, I have assumed his favorite position: on my back, left arm extended and bent at a right angle, creating a warm corral for him to knead and recline in, chin resting on my forearm as he leans back against my upper arm. I guess I assume this position naturally now, perhaps responding unconsciously to his prompting at some predawn hour, perhaps flipping onto my back when I hear the light *click-click-click* of his toenails on the wood floor. Whatever the reason, it is early yet when I awake this time, and I can close my eyes again and enjoy the warm presence of his body leaning into mine awhile longer. I sleep again, sweet and dreamless, and when I wake to the buzz of Jon's alarm, I try not to move, savoring still the cat's presence next to me. And then Jon rouses himself, sits and then stands up, reaching for a towel as he lumbers in his own sweet way to the door. And then Cyrus stands too, stretches with his back arched like the best of Halloween cats, and follows him down the hall. My men. Normal life continues, at least for now. I let my eyes close again for a moment, then push myself out of the covers to open a can of cat food, to check the coffee, to start my day.

For most of us, truth be told, cohabiting with cats is nearly pure pleasure and a selfish pleasure at that. We do it for what we get out of it—the purr, the sight of an upturned chin as our feline companion flips to sleep with his head upside down, the cool feel of those tiny fangs as he goes on "autopet"—brushing himself against us and marking us as his own with a swipe of his head. And we can be at ease with this selfishness because it seems so much a part of the relationship, so reciprocal. This is the upside of our pets' much vaunted self-possession. We know they're getting something out of it also, or they would leave or, at least, find a destructive way of letting us know. They are cats, after all. Self-fulfillment is part of their job.

There comes a time, though, when even the most selfish of us must put our pets' needs first. When letting go and doing the right thing may hurt us more than we'd ever imagined. When we must make the hard choices and forego the selfishness of our pleasure with their company, and give them peace.

Sometimes, it is easier than others. All of us who have loved our pets throughout their lives hope for this kind of ending, pray that one morning our aged and ailing pets will just not respond and we will find them, curled into their perfect discs of relaxation, only this time cool and still. Some of us find it, but such cases are rare. I've not found any studies on unassisted, natural death in pet cats, but in my informal survey I heard of only two such cases among more than two dozen.

More of us will find that the time comes when we must euthanize our pets, and that decision is rarely easy.

"We moved, and it was a move I did not want to make," remembers Juli. "I made it because my husband wanted to, so it was difficult for me as it was. And it seemed pretty soon after that Sophie started getting sick."

The beginning of the end for Juli's petite pink-nosed cat came, she says, when Sophie developed some kind of a virus that inflamed her mouth and throat and made eating difficult. "It became a nightly ritual of finding something for her to eat, and shots and prednisone, and incredible weight loss. She was just miserable and it was really sad," says the usually vivacious blonde. "Other than her mouth, it seemed like she was fine," she says, but the inability to eat began to drain the little cat. "At the end, I was tying a napkin around her and force-feeding her baby food. Feeding her was an event every night."

As so many of us have experienced, there were periods of remission. Juli would begin to grow hopeful. Her cat, after all, wasn't yet fifteen years old. "She would gain weight and I'd be really excited," she recalls. The rally never lasted.

"She was down to five pounds; her eyes were glazed. There

was a one-week period when, if I even got her to eat something, she would throw it up. I couldn't even tell anymore what she was eating, what she wasn't." Juli pauses. Almost a year later, she still tears up. "One night I put her on the table and said, 'All right, Soph, time to eat,' and we cuddled for a while and tried to eat. About half an hour or an hour later, I noticed her trying to get up the stairs. Her back legs kept collapsing under her. She went under the stairs and tried to hide, and I went and I lay next to her. She was breathing very heavily, and I thought, 'Okay, this is it.'

"I had made many pacts with Sophie," Juli recalls, remembering them all. "It was like, 'Hang in there. You promised me.' I bargained with Sophie a lot, mostly asking her to hang in there until I had a baby, which I figured would be another two years. I also felt kind of ripped off by the whole ordeal. I know so many people who had their cats for sixteen to twenty years and I felt like it was my shitty luck to only have Sophie for fourteen."

That night, Juli released Sophie: "I was just like: 'The bets are off. You can go.' I wish she could have just died then, but it's never that easy. I was saying, 'You can go, it's all right.' And then I realized I had to take her to the vet. Part of me was a little bit relieved, all this was over." Nearly a year of hand feeding her had been difficult. "I couldn't leave for business trips. I couldn't have anyone else feed her. She wouldn't eat."

She took Sophie to the animal hospital's emergency room. Then, as is often the case, nothing seemed clear anymore. "They took X rays and her temperature was pretty high. But they gave her a shot and some fluid, and they said we can keep her overnight or you can take her home. So I brought her home and laid her on the couch and brought her a little water. And then I went to clean up the kitchen and she had moved herself, so I got excited but then I saw she was breathing really, really heavily. So I called a cab and we went back to the hospital, and they took her temperature again and it was higher, and I was like, 'Okay, I'm ready.' They put her on the table and I looked at her face and petted her head and that was it."

Sophie's final illness, says Juli, was perhaps the most difficult passage she has yet experienced. It was not, however, without its gifts. "I know I learned an incredible amount about patience, just about my nurturing side, about loyalty and stability," she says. "I never thought that I would be able to sit there and feed something twice a day. It was really interesting to step back and see myself as a caretaker: Sophie needs shots twice a month, I'll give up my fake nails to pay for them. I love my fake nails, but this is what a mommy does."

As a vet at Angell Memorial, Dr. Jean Duddy sees many of her patients and their owners through this most difficult transition. "As we get older, one of the last big lessons we learn is the process of grieving," says the large hearty woman. "It's hard, especially for single pet owners. Single cat owners are probably the worst affected by it." The options for continuing care, she says, don't make the end any easier. When do you try exploratory surgery or a kidney transplant, both of which are available for cats? When do you hydrate or stop hydrating? In some ways, and I say this as someone who has done both, knowing you have the power to end your pet's life can be harder than watching a loved human die. "With humans you don't have choices, with cats you do," Duddy points out. "It goes along with being a cat owner."

That last decision, she says, is so often the hardest. Part of her job is to make it easier. "I use the corniest line: 'You'll know,' I say. Most people come in and tell me, 'I knew.' Cats in general are very good at telling us. They do it through subtle ways. They'll stop eating. They'll let you know: 'I'm not feeling well; I don't want you to touch me anymore.' Or I'll hear, 'God they had a great day and then just crashed.' I do believe in the last hurrah. I think the animals do that—there are a lot of animals out there who I honestly believe wait till the owner can deal with the death and then they go, 'Okay, I can go.' "

As a pet owner, Duddy has her own experience of loss. "I swear my cat was waiting until I got home," she remembers. "She'd been failing and I was just about ready to make the decision and I came home and she came over to me and sat in my lap, and I could tell that she was going to die that night. And I pretty much sat there with her, and she didn't seem to be in any pain. When I had been there for a few hours with her, I decided maybe I should put her to sleep. She died in my lap on the way to the hospital, in the car on the way to the hospital."

For many of us, this final period brings sweetness as well as pain. Harvey, Laura's adored misfit, developed liver disease when he was about twelve years old, and she remembers how the opportunity to care for her cat through his final illness gave her the opportunity to show her love.

"There's a settee in the backyard, and that was his favorite spot his whole life," she says, remembering the affectionate, floppy cat. "At the end, he was very weak. He didn't have energy to walk very well. He lost his appetite; I was feeding him baby food. But he wanted to go sit in his spot, so I'd let him outside and it would take almost an hour to get from the back door to his spot. He'd walk a few steps, and then he'd sit down and rest, and then he'd walk a few steps, and then sit and rest. The next day it would take him longer, and he was eating less.

"By midweek, it was almost like we were reading each other's minds. I would take him to his spot. And then he'd want to go to the shade, so I'd take him. Then he'd want to pee, so I'd hold him up. He stopped drinking, and his favorite place to drink had been the drip out of the faucet in the bathtub, so I went and sat in the bathtub with him in my arms so he could drink from the faucet. And the way he looked at me, the love, was the thank-you.

"He wasn't howling, he was just slow. And he got weaker and weaker. I was going to have him put down, and one friend in particular told me that Harvey would tell me when it was time. We'd go to the vet, and I'd put him on the table, and he'd perk up. And I thought, 'No, it's not time.' Two days later, he was so weak that I basically had to carry him around. He couldn't even hold his head up. I thought, 'Who knows? Maybe it's one more day.' I was in the habit of putting him on the bed. That night he didn't want to be on the bed, so I put him down with the other cats in the front room. I'm very sensitive to him. I'd sleep a bit, then I'd wake up and go to him. It was the middle of the night and I heard him and I woke up, and he had dragged himself from the living room into my bedroom and he was standing there, shaking and meowing for me. It wasn't like a pain meow, but he wanted something. So I scooped him up and brought him up on the bed and I have never in my life felt so much love from an animal as I did at that moment. It was amazing to me.

"That was our last night, and in the morning, he told me. He started howling. And so then we went into the vet. I held him in my arms while the vet gave him the shot, and then I brought him home." Harvey is now buried in the backyard, near his favorite spot.

JANUARY

For me, the decision has been as awful as I'd feared, made worse by the seeming ebb and flow of my kitty's mood and behavior. In truth, it's been a long time coming, probably because for so long I refused to see the damage time and illness—diseases of his kidneys and his bowels—had wrought. I don't remember, for example, when I started hearing the click of his nails on the wood floor, or what I told myself when I did. As he sleeps on his chair, as he does most of the day, I can see why I hear them: either because of dehydration or the wasting of his muscles, he no longer retracts his claws.

On the Monday night when he fell over while walking away from his water dish, I was distraught but convinced. I ran to him as he pulled himself almost upright, and when he crawled under the kitchen table, I told myself, "This is no kind of a life." I put down a folded tablecloth for a bed and gently lifted him onto it and sat by him. He roused and walked off to one of his more usual and carpeted haunts, but though I followed him choked and nauseous with tears, I thought, "This is the time. This is clear." My husband and I cried together that night, as we hand-fed our pet bits of sliced turkey and baby food and watched him slowly slump off to the cat bed in my office. Although we didn't admit it to each other until later, we both prayed that night that he would die in his sleep before we awoke. Imagine our surprise when, in the predawn hours, I felt a familiar soft thud. Cyrus had hopped onto the bed by my side, and was waiting for me to extend my arm to make a nest for him. I did and he kneaded my arm and lay down, chin resting on my forearm, as if nothing had happened. I slept much more easily for the rest of the morning, and I had to fight back my own urge to not call the vet.

This, however, was serious, even if not the end, and so I did call Melissa. "Maybe it's nothing," I said to her, trying to believe it. We got an appointment for the next afternoon, and the following thirty hours were hell. "This is not a cat who has given up on life," I e-mailed Jon, reporting that Cyrus had sauntered off to use his litter box and stopped for a snack and a drink on the way back. "Maybe it is time," I messaged later, when he again stumbled and fell, even the shortened jump from the bed to the footstool I had placed by its side too much for his overburdened system. "We'll see what the vet says," we kept promising each other, but that night when he joined us on the couch as of old, kneading my lap and purring during the nightly repeat of *Law and Order* I thought, "He's not ready yet." The truth may have been that I wasn't.

Speaking some things aloud seemed to help. I remembered what Juli had told me about "releasing" Sophie from her obligations and tried it myself. "I understand if you can't help me finish this book," I told my cat, as he lay on his chair. "You don't have to, it's okay." I told him I would dedicate this book to him, and that he had been a marvelous cat, the best friend and companion I could have ever wanted. "Yes, you have. Yes, you have," I repeated, in the mantralike way Jon and I had adopted for speaking to our darling years before.

I e-mailed Juli, who understood immediately.

"I always said to Sophie 'Do you promise to be my kitten for-ever?' " she responded. "Of course she is, even though she's not here with me. I know someone I love is taking care of her (maybe being bitten) right now. It's hokey but I imagine Alberta, my childhood nanny, caring for her until I meet her in the great beyond. Wow, I guess having her made me believe in the after-life, or at least helped me identify that I do.

"Anyway there's not much I can say that will make you feel better except do all the dumb things you think are right," she advised. "Make promises. Take pictures. Buy him a tuna steak. If indeed the time is right you'll know it and I think he'd thank you for letting him go if he could."

"I am so sorry to hear about little Cyrus," wrote Cynthia, the cat-sheltering artist, when I messaged her. "Good luck with the vet tomorrow. If he is suffering it is best to put him gently to sleep and ease his pain. I did not do so with Olympus, my cat with a tumor, and his death was stressful and hard on him. I vowed that next time I will not be so selfish and try to keep my little sick ones with me at the cost of their own suffering. My heart goes out to you and Jon. Cyrus is a beautiful little fellow. Please give him a pat and kiss for me!"

🐾

Jon came home early the next afternoon, in time for our vet appointment. Melissa knew we were scared and used her gentlest voice when she asked if we wanted to put him to sleep. I told her that we just weren't sure. That was, she said, the answer she had expected. "I wouldn't have advised doing it today anyway. You need time to prepare, even if it's just a few days," she told us, once she had examined him. We agreed to hydrate him, but not to put him on the prednisone, a steroid that might have helped his bowels, but at the cost of his kidneys. He had, probably, at best a few weeks left—Melissa murmured assent when I said this—and the idea of forcing medicine, even in liquid form, down his throat seemed a poor way to spend that time. "You keep him around for as long as you need to," she continued. "He's going to be okay, so don't worry about that. This is a time when you can be a little selfish."

Melissa left us with a practical suggestion: we would get a calendar and start marking which days were good, which bad, so that we would have some objective sense of when the bad ones outweighed the good. And when she left I felt, at first, much better. "Our kitty is still with us!" I rejoiced, before getting clobbered by the full weight of "My kitty is dying." When I see him settle down before his food dish or, increasingly, by the water bowl, he moves slowly, as if every bend cost him. When I pet him, ever so gently, he is all fur and bones and spirit, his green eyes glowing at me.

🐾

As he is losing his battle, I am losing my fantasies. Let's face it: I have long seen my cat as he would be were he human, a kind of gallant Puss in Boots, a cavalier-type feline, his heroic role augmented by his lush ruff and tail plumage. He has been the statesman, the hunter, always the sophisticate.

In my sleep, I know that this is not the truth. I recall the night, several weeks ago, when I woke and reached for Cyrus, seeking to pet the purr. My hand connected with fur and sharpness, the hollow of bones, the knobs of spine. "This is not a cat," I thought, before waking enough to recognize my pet. Even in half sleep, I know.

Increasingly, these days, I must remind myself that Cyrus is not my projections. He is an animal. And I am trying to learn to respect that, to not urge him to eat simply because I cannot stand seeing that he is bone thin. To not encourage him to jump off the bed when I know he wants his rest. I want to make him sprightly again, to force him to romp, and of course I cannot. It's very hard to do, to let go of the fantasy and let the animal be. To simply love the little beastie as he is.

JANUARY 24, 2001

After a bad day in which he ate little and did little but stagger from his chair to his litter box to pee out all the fluid that had been given him from the drip bag under his skin, and then slowly make his way back again to sleep, we decided to call Melissa and have her come to do it tomorrow. Immediately after, of course,

Cyrus staggered—there's just no other word—into the living room and we fed him some baby food there and had a big cry. And last night, for the first time in days, he made it up to the bed (I have a pillow as well as the footstool set up as steps) and he kneaded my arm and slept with us, for a while. He has such a will! But his body is just so weak, and it hurts to see him wobbling. It's not just "creaky old cat with a limp" time now. He's wobbly and slow and he looks like every movement is an effort. When he does go to eat he has trouble bending over and sitting down. And this is one of the good times. He was just hydrated yesterday.

I think we're making the right decision, but it's hard to be sure. It's so hard anyway. He's being so good, still struggling to the litter box (which makes me convinced that all those "accidents" over the years were really intentional). He's eating for now; I'd made a green mark on the calendar in the kitchen yesterday. But either today or tomorrow, unless we rehydrate him, that would stop and the constipation would kick in again, a blockage so bad that he vomits whenever he tries to force out one hard dry turd. I think about the subcutaneous hydration, the minutes of drip, the big needle. To rehydrate him again for so small a return really seems like just prolonging the agony. The rewards, I tell myself, are diminishing.

The problem is, in part, that he's such a fierce kitty. He doesn't want to just stay still and rest. He wants to walk to the living room or the litter box or the food (I have food and water in his office, as I now think of my office, but he still walks to the kitchen a lot of the time). He'll let me spoon feed him, which I've been doing for the last week or so. But then he wants to walk to the kitchen anyway, and it's so hard to see him slowly, weakly going for a bit and then pausing, sometimes just lying on the cold floor.

I guess I would feel better, more sure of this decision, if he couldn't walk anymore, or didn't leave his chair for twenty-four hours (he's stayed there for twelve at least) or soiled himself (he doesn't clean himself anymore, but doesn't pee on himself either). But if we wait till that happens—and it probably would happen soon—not only would we be wrecks, I would know that we'd waited too long, like Cynthia said she waited too long watching her big old boy Olympus as he tried to hide from his own pain. It's just hard. Am I merely justifying our decision to end our own agony? Probably. But I like to think Cyrus understands.

Amy had an equally tough time, she tells Jon, and Jon passes her e-mail along to me. I can't talk to anyone, but I can read. "One of the things that really helped me decide about Daphne was when the vet reminded me that she wouldn't know what was happening," she wrote. "It was still awful, but I kept trying to remember that. And what a great life she'd had."

JANUARY 25, 2001:

Well, our dear kitty—the sixteen-year-old perfect master—is gone. It was as good as it could be. He spent the last night with us. First he dragged himself into the living room and we lifted him onto the couch and he crawled onto my lap and purred. Then we took him to bed with us and he spent most of the night there. He even kneaded my arm weakly. At around 5 A.M., he wanted to get down. He tried to walk to the foot of the bed where the steps were for him, but he fell over. I pulled him back from the edge so he wouldn't fall off and soon he tried again, so I helped him down to the carpet and he made his proud, stiff way back to his bed in the office, slow drag by slow drag by slow drag. Most of the morning we sat with him. He came out of his bed and ate a little, drank a little, lying on the rug. Then he dragged himself back into his bed, and we sat with him.

At two o'clock, Melissa came. Cyrus was so weak, he was like a warm doll when Jon picked him up out of his bed and brought him into the living room and handed him to me. We sat on the living room floor with him, and he growled at Melissa just like old times, only a little softer. I looked away as she gave him the first shot, to sedate him, and then we sat holding him for a while. First I held him and Jon held both of us, then I passed him to Jon who held him awhile, and we both kissed him and talked to him. He was unconscious, floppy as a rag doll, but still warm, still our kitty. Then Jon handed him back to me and Melissa gave him the shot that stopped his heart and I held him and Jon petted him and I felt his pounding heart slow and stop. Melissa then left us alone for a while, and we held his little body and cried and said good-bye again.

We went out for a long walk after Melissa left (she took him for cremation), stopping finally for a beer and some food and later, the movie *Chocolat*. Don't ask if it was good or not, and don't read further if you plan on seeing it. All I can tell you for certain is that Judi Dench's character had a cat, a fine, healthy cat, and that made me cry. I think Jon was crying too. Then Judi Dench died, and we both bawled out loud. I think the cat was okay, although I don't clearly remember if you see him again or not, and I never want to see that movie again.

Coming home was terrible. Going to bed without him was terrible. As I write this it's the next day, and that's terrible too. He was the perfect companion, so much personality in such a little package.

11

THE SOLACE OF CATS

"Having a cat has taught me humility," says Helen quietly, as she pours the hot water into the teapot. She has already tried to coax Moses, her fifteen-year-old companion, out to greet me, with no luck. "Dogs, as they say, have owners. Cats have attendants."

At eighty-four, Helen has clearly also learned patience. Soon after we sit down to discuss the relationship she has carried on with the handsome calico, Moses appears. A small, plump female, discovered as a homeless kitten and named for the great biblical foundling, Moses sniffs my outstretched hand daintily and retires to a nearby settee, or "settle" as Helen calls it, to wash and resume her afternoon napping. "You're such a good little companion," Helen says to her, while we wait for the Earl Gray to steep. "She came to us having been very well brought up," she explains, and begins her story.

Despite living alone all her adult life, Helen has never really felt lonely. One of four children raised on a large upstate New York farm, she'd been brought up to be self-sufficient and to trust in ties that reached across distances. "I went away to school at the age of seventeen," she says; that was what the family expected. Although her sister and two brothers then pursued lives in cities around the country, they retained a strong sense of family. "We were very closely knit, and always have been."

When Helen found herself in Boston, pursuing a career in nursing, she didn't seek to replace her family. She did, however, need more than her work. "I didn't know a soul," she recalls. She enjoyed her church, "and that was great as far as it went." But it was the Appalachian Mountain Club that finally won the majority of her free time, if not her heart. With the club, Helen's independence became an asset to be treasured. "I was free to go hiking on weekends or for a week at a time or to travel. That was the thing: the freedom! And then when I got a car, that made further exploration possible."

Until her stepmother called with her story of the stray kitten, Helen had never thought of a pet. At sixty-nine, after years of nursing and teaching, she had not wanted the responsibility of caring for another creature. But the call from her stepmother carried a sense of urgency. Nearly blind, her widowed step-mother shared the family farmhouse with two cats and a dog already; one more cat seemed too much of a burden. And the kit-ten who had been mewing by her door clearly wanted to be let in, clearly wanted to be a house cat, and had probably been one before being abandoned or lost in the the wide-open county of farms and woods.

"She had such impeccable manners," recalls Helen, noting that the kitten had obviously had a caring mother and most probably some human companionship before its journey to her stepmother's. But still, a pet meant a commitment, a loss of free-dom and mobility. "I cried all night the night before I went to take that kitten home," Helen remembers now. "I didn't want the responsibility."

Fifteen years later she has no regrets. First and foremost, she discovered that her young cat could do quite well with a pet-sitter; preferred, in fact, for someone to drop by twice a day rather than to be carried along on Helen's weekend excursions. ("She got car sick," Helen confesses. Moses wakes up and eyes me, tail twitching.) And then, too, she learned to love the rotund calico, perhaps more so as the two aged together and her own gait became unsteady.

Helen doesn't hike through the mountains anymore. "I wobble quite a bit, you know," she admits. Still, she walks several hours a day. "It's important, and it gets me out to see people. And then I come back to this little one." She looks over at the sleeping feline with obvious affection.

"You want different things at different times of your life, I've discovered," she notes. "And the discovery has been quite pleasant."

The solace of cats for many of us begins at home. We've heard of their empathy, the way they seem to sense our needs at particular times and respond with warm comfort, with gentler than usual behavior. Sometimes, just having a cat to love can be enough.

For Ruth, the comfort worked both ways. An Icelandic immigrant now living in Los Angeles, the short, muscular masseuse didn't hear about her grandmother's death until two days after the fact. "She was over in Europe," she explains the delay—and the crisis that propelled her into cat ownership four years ago, her slight Nordic accent flattening the emotion in her borrowed English. "But I felt terrible that I hadn't heard right away. I went out for breakfast that morning, when I did, and I came back and passed this pet place. 'Pet Adoptions,' it said, and I thought, 'Oh, I'm going to go look at the animals.' "

She had no intention, that March morning, of adopting one. The cats and her sudden loss, however, acted their own magic. "I picked one up and he threw his arms around me, around my neck. And in that moment there was no longer any question that I wasn't going to take him home," she says of the black-and-white Manuel. "And I thought, 'He can't be alone. I need a companion for him' " Looking through the other cages set up by the rescue group in charge, she saw one that was covered up, hidden away, and she asked about it. "They said, 'Oh, you don't want to see her. She's really mean and she hates people.' " That answer only intrigued Ruth, and she pressed to be shown the feral female inside. "There was this little creature," she recalls. "Undernourished, filthy, completely asocial. She wanted nothing to do with the world. Of course, I took her home."

Following the advice of the rescue workers, Ruth set out to socialize her undersized tabby with the bright green eyes. Wrapping her in a towel to stop her struggling, she held her several times a day, and otherwise let her hide in the bathroom, where she had her own food and water dishes and litter box. By the fourth day, Zina—named for the green-eyed refugee heroine of a movie—had stopped struggling. "She was my happy camper," says the similarly green-eyed woman, who has since built her two cats a multistory castle in her apartment.

The effort has paid off many times over. "They are very therapeutic to be around," observes Ruth, with the calm appraisal of an athlete. "They force me to be very present with them. Everyday they are thrilled when I play with them. Everyday they are excited when I feed them. I love the routine of getting up and feeding them. He asks for food in the morning; she asks for food at night. In difficult times in my life, they are such a comfort. They are consistently wonderful and consistently present."

For myself, in the weeks following Cyrus's death, I find it at times trying, at other times a great consolation to be around cats, to talk to women about their cats, to pet healthy, sleek cats.

Sometimes, it's too much, and more than once I've come home from an interview to burst out crying in the privacy of my kitchen. I'm sure I seemed distracted and inattentive to the women I had just left, and I send them my belated apologies.

Sometimes, being home is too much. I keep looking for Cyrus. I've read about phantom-limb syndrome, during which people feel pain in an amputated limb. I have phantom-cat syndrome. Jon seems to suffer from it also. Sometimes he yells out "Kitty!" as he wanders around at night, looking for his slippers or yet another misplaced CD. He says this is just habit, but I think it comforts him to do so, so I don't tell him how much it hurts me. "Kitty!"

There are other losses, of course, and I feel self-conscious about how hard this one has hit me. I think about Helen, and the peace she has found with Moses, and I ponder how cats comfort us. How the presence of a cat can help us face the inevitable deprivations of time, as we age, as we lose our health or those around us. I think we gravitate to them instinctively at such times, holding on to life as we cling to their soft and often pliant selves. They bring us back to earth, back to our sensual selves, back to our healthiest parts.

Even in our prime, they're a source of solace. Jeanne has just been promoted again, but this time around, the slim, hard-working journalist says she's going to try to keep in mind the lesson her cats, Joop and Jeffrey, provide. "They add a routine in our life that's not bad to have. They're a good model for me," she says during a hurried morning break. The tortoiseshell Jeffrey looks like a fluffy pushover, but he can get very loud when he wants his breakfast, she explains. And Joop, whose gray-and-white markings belong more to a purebred Maine coon than a shelter stray, keeps Jeanne in line with his own routine: first food, then water, then belly rubs. "And if I try to pet him before I give him his sink water, he jumps up and runs to the sink. He thinks I'm a little stupid."

Before these two, and their predecessor, Jasper, came into Jeanne's life, she didn't have much by way of daily rituals at all. "I have the kind of addictive personality where I could easily stop taking care of myself. I get out of the habit," she says. "I'm always rushing, I'm always falling into bed when I'm dead tired. I go six months between haircuts because there's no time for me.

"When we got the cats, I was afraid of the responsibility of having them. But certain tasks are good, they add normalcy. These guys are a good model for putting your needs first in a healthy way. Plus, they remind me that it's okay to ask for what you want."

Some of us take this application further, bringing our cats into caregiving situations for the comfort they bring. There is nothing specifically gender oriented about such work, about the visits that cats and their people pay to nursing homes or assisted-living residences. This work, which is usually called pet-assisted therapy, is simply a somewhat more passive version of what seeing-eye or hearing dogs have been doing for years, in a way, using their healthy senses to aid ailing humans. For although many of us have stories of how our cats have alerted us to danger or invaders or even fire, most of us recognize that the primary benefit the presence of a cat confers is simply its company, soothing and placid.

There is nothing specifically female about health care, either, a fact that should become obvious to anyone who has ever perused the ratio of female to male doctors at a major metropolitan hospital. Consider, however, the preponderance of women in the nurturing professions—the nurses and aides, the social workers and home health-care providers who often fill in the human side after the technology of medicine has done its work—and a connection begins to emerge. Some of this is due to historical bias and is being redressed, of course, as more women enter specialized fields of medicine and research. And much of it is the result of subtler injustices, as working mothers and less fortunate daughters were shunted into these less profitable, less "important" professions. Much of it may, as well, be the result of how the mix of socialization and expectation has led us to become the ones who focus on relationships, who rely on chats and hugs as much as on serums and pills, and who are willing to consider nontraditional therapies and non-Western medicines. For all these reasons, women still hold up more than half the hard duty of patient care. And therefore it should come as no surprise that we are the pioneers in pet-assisted therapy.

While hard numbers don't exist, the anecdotal evidence shows our worth: Women are the ones who answer the ads from nursing homes, like Michelle of Blakkatz Cattery does, bringing our cats around to console the arthritic and bedridden. We are the ones who make up roughly 90 percent of the volunteers for groups like the Washington-based Delta Society, according to officials in this group, which trains and places pet and people teams for animal-assisted therapy and animal-assisted activities with the disabled and the elderly. We are the ones, like Donna Francis, whose one-eyed cat Lucky was given the Delta Society's 2000 Beyond Limits Award, whose animals provide encouragement and companionship; in this case, motivating hearing-impaired children to grow beyond the shyness imposed by their disability.

Although they remain in the minority (composing only about 130 of the 4,000 Delta Society animals), our cats are making a difference. The beneficial effects that pets have on our blood pressure has become fairly common knowledge: a 1999 study at the State University of New York at Buffalo finally confirmed the anecdotal evidence by measuring how much pressure and triglyceride levels were lowered in those who cohabit with either cats or dogs. According to another study, by Richard Avanzino, the presence of a pet can also help ground psychiatric patients, even those with severe disorders such as schizophrenia and bipolar disorder (manic depression). Avanzino served as the president of the San Francisco Society for the Prevention of Cruelty to Animals, which conducted sixty-five visits by animals to a locked psychiatric unit of San Francisco General Hospital over a three-year period from 1984 to 1987. The results, he reported, were striking: more than 45 percent of the patients showed improved socialization, more than 43 percent increased their communication, and 33 percent became more oriented toward reality after visits from shelter animals. These visits, by dogs, cats, and other small animals, were bringing these patients back.

Dogs continue to make up the bulk of therapy animals. They can be trained to guide, to respond, and to guard. But cats are contributing to these advances as well, as those of us who love them are learning to exploit their natural behavior in therapeutic settings. For our cats, such work may simply be an extension of their lifelong interest in us.

Sushi, for example, was long used to being a professional cat. A classic sealpoint Siamese with dark chocolate ears, Sushi, at the ripe age of fourteen, has only recently retired from the show circuit. A lush and shapely cream, she has also served as the Sheba Cat Foods cat of the year, and has always been a very sociable kitty. "She's very sweet and laid-back," her owner, Sherry, tells me, stroking the sleek café au lait back. Therefore, when Sherry read an ad in her local Rhode Island newspaper three years ago calling for "well-behaved cats and kittens," this second career seemed like a natural progression.

For Sushi, after more than a decade of being primped and posing, the interview with the nursing home's recreation director was a snap. "The recreation director sat on the floor with her and let her explore," recalls Sherry. "She warmed right up to it, crawled over everything, so the director picked her up and said, 'Okay, let's go meet the people.' "

That's where Sushi showed her true championship qualities. "Before I could say, 'Hi, we're Sherry and Sushi,' she went up to one woman who was asleep in her wheelchair. Her hands were hanging over the side, and Sushi walked underneath her hand and lifted her head so she was touching the person. The woman opened her eyes and started smiling and talking to Sushi, and Sushi started purring.

"From the minute she walked in, she wasn't afraid of the people, of the smells or the different apparatuses," says Sherry proudly, although she does admit that, for unknown reasons, Sushi has been a bit wary of a recliner on the home's second floor. The result—as long as her friends are not in that one chair—has been a strong bond with the residents. And although Sushi does not perform the utilitarian functions that a guide dog might, she works with the residents in other ways. She's a nonjudgmental visitor who can encourage stroke victims to pet her and talk to her. She brings depressed people out of themselves, at least temporarily, and gives the pleasure of a purr and soft fur to those who have become weighed down by their illnesses and age.

These days, Sushi, accompanied by Sherry, visits two nursing homes each week, spending several hours with the residents. Often the visits are quite a bit of fun. "We dress her up for the holidays," says Sherry, talking about the Santa hat that Sushi dons and the reindeer antlers that her younger colleague, Ling Ling, is willing to accept for seasonal amusement. "Everyone gets a kick out of it."

Such joys are by their nature fleeting, however, and Sushi has lost her share of nursing home friends. Sherry remembers one woman, coming in and out of a coma, who shared her sorrow and her comfort with the glossy cat. "She said, 'I love you, Sushi, and I wanted to say good-bye, I won't be here next week.' And then she went back out. The family was crying, the tears were rolling down my face. Sushi looked at her, and just nuzzled close to her.

"It seems like animals always touch a sensitive spot in people," muses Sherry. "There was a retired professor from Brown University who had lost his wife and was very sad. And Sushi got him to talk. He would talk French and she seemed to understand, and they'd listen to classical music together. He's failing now, and we went in last week. He didn't remember me, but he remembered Sushi immediately."

In the process, Sushi has also taught much about herself to Sherry. "I thought, this will be a different thing for her, not sitting in her cage, being out with people."

In retrospect, says Sherry, she should have realized that Sushi had a nurturing side. The cat owner recalls how, after she had major abdominal surgery twelve years ago, Sushi became more attentive. "She never left my side," Sherry recalls. "She lay on the incision and purred, and I found it very soothing."

Now, she says, "I realize she was showing me a different side of her from the show-cat side, but it takes a human a lot longer to catch on. That was years before we set foot in a nursing home. She had to teach me, to get me to this point, where I would take her somewhere where she could do this. Humans are such slow learners."

There's so much we could share, if we were willing to. One month after Cyrus died, when I was finally getting back to work on this project, I called Diane to ask about her cats, in particular nineteen-year-old Rossi. She apologized for not getting back to me sooner. Her mother-in-law had had a stroke and was probably dying, and it seemed that Rossi was declining as well. She was keeping up his medications, but was beginning to think about learning to hydrate him. "He drinks so much," she told me. I thought of my own experience with those last days, of my own denial, and didn't respond. She was also behind in her writing assignments, she told me, and hadn't yet been able to bring herself to review a new memoir, *Waiting for My Cats to Die*, by Stacy Horn, that she had taken on. We chatted briefly about the possible reasons for her reluctance to finish this project and then signed off. Giving her my sympathy and love, I realized that I'd already progressed beyond the worst of it.

Moving on is hard. "After Oscar died, I thought that I would not get a cat for a couple of months at least, just to embrace my catless existence in some Zen-like manner," said Kyoko, remembering the sudden illness and demise of her last cat. "I told my friends, 'I've never really lived alone. I've had a cat since I was twenty-two.' It was time."

After a few weeks, however, the catlessness began to wear on the novelist. "I was walking down the street and I was thinking if a truck came by and hit me it would be no big deal." Upon hearing that, her boyfriend—who had three felines of his own—said, "You need your own cat again."

"It was true. I hated coming back to a catless apartment at the end of the day. I really feared coming up here." She gestures to the cozy sunlit room where she and I sit drinking tea with her two current Siamese. "And I decided that Oscar would not want me to be alone: I could never replace him, but I could address my catlessness.

"I considered going to the humane shelter, but I've always really liked Siamese cats, so I started calling all the breeders around here. They were all out of town or else they had no kittens available. I ended up calling some breeders in Wisconsin," where she had previously studied, "thinking that I'd go visit some friends, pick up a cat, and fly back. One of the breeders said that she had one ready to go. She had been saving him for another breeder, but this other breeder had backed out of the deal and now the cat was there with nowhere to go. She shipped him to me. I went to meet my cat, Ernest, at the airport. He was delayed because he could not be shipped on the earlier flight—it was too hot. So I had to spend three hours at the airport waiting for him and he came after midnight. He was kind of upset about the whole travel thing so he hid under the bed for two days. Then he came out and we started sitting on the couch together and then we started sleeping together. I slept on the couch for the first two days because that's where he seemed to want to sleep. Then we moved to the bed. Somewhere along in there, I realized that we now understood each other. About the fourth day, when I came home from being away at work, he was sitting on the couch and he meowed and meowed as if to say that I should have come home earlier. Maybe that was the moment when I knew that we had a life together."

Her small apartment still seemed lacking, however. She looked into feng shui and considered redecorating, although with one wall of windows and another broken by a fireplace there wasn't much she could do. Finally, realization hit: "I didn't want to rearrange my furniture. I wanted another cat!" Finding Algernon was easier, because by then a friend had met a reliable local breeder. Within days, the two kittens had progressed from hissing to grooming each other. As we talk, they sleep curled together, a brown and gray version of a yin-yang symbol. "Now I feel like I have the two right cats," Kyoko says. Her house is filled with warm energy once more.

With some trepidation, I got a copy of Stacy Horn's book. Looking at pictures of Cyrus could still make me tear up, and every time I opened a CD or cassette and realized I didn't have to hide the shrink wrap to keep him from devouring it (and promptly vomiting) was a little heartbreak. I found Horn's memoir of life with two diabetic cats darkly funny—Horn is even more morbid than I—and began to experience a distant sense of companionship. I prefer cooking as therapy, rather than graveyard visiting, but to each her own. Once again with us cat women, it's our commonalities that draw us together.

Somewhere in the midst of all this, I heard from Juli. She and Brad had adopted brother and sister kittens, whom they named Ike and Tina. "I didn't even want a cat for about six months," her e-mail told me. Their Webcam showed two somewhat grainy fuzz balls curled up by Brad's guitar case. Not too clear, but clearly loved. "At about eight months, I just kind of knew."

For Amy, cats seem to come in a progression. Daphne, she tells me, was her first cat. But Luigi was, perhaps, her first real love, a glossy black kitten she raised herself. She'd adopted the oddly marked Sophie ("part Siamese, part hedgehog") to keep him company, and the squat, brown-eared, gray-striped female seemed to amuse them both. But when Luigi died suddenly, suffering apparent heart failure during a car ride, Sophie was no comfort to Amy. "I wanted Luigi back. I wanted it to have been her that died," she admits.

Sophie seemed to miss Luigi as well, and would wander from room to room in the sprawling third-floor flat looking for her playmate. Finally, Amy broke down. "I just couldn't stand having only one cat," she says in retrospect. Thus, Ernie, a tabby tom, joined the family, and although Amy loves his round face and his penchant for hiding in boxes, she's begun to feel that Sophie's especially discriminating affection merits more of her attention. "Now she's the special one," she says, talking about Sophie, who has now also been dubbed "the Prime Minister."

Then Amy suffered two losses. Daphne, who had been living with her parents, had to be put to sleep when her cancer came back, and a long-term relationship broke up. "He was always down on my idea of getting another kitten," she says of her former boyfriend. "So I thought, 'I'm going to go out and get a third one!'"

Mrs. Margaret Dumont, the household's latest addition, is curled on her cat bed when I visit. Six months in, the fat black cat (who has, Amy points out, a bit of dandruff) hasn't quite settled in with her feline partners. But she kneads the black plush blanket and leans back with pleasure as I brush her, a roll of fat appearing in the glossy fur behind her neck. "She was apparently totally feral several months before I adopted her," says Amy of the cat who looks to be at least part seal. More than one of us, it seems, can experience a second chance at love.

Increasingly, as the months go by, people are suggesting that for me and for Jon the time is right.

"It's a bright spot in a sad moment to have a bitty kit bouncing around, and also sort of circular in that the new arrival can still recognize the presence of the old one if she arrives soon enough," says Erin. "You can follow her around as she smells all the corners and say, 'Yup, that was Puddinhead, and she was dear and strong and sometimes bitchy and that was the corner where she'd pee when she was mad, but I loved her very much anyway and now I love you, too—though you'd better not pee in the corners.' And then she will anyway and you know you'll be okay."

In early March, we go to Texas and close-dance at the Broken Spoke. We eat barbecue, and buy cowboy boots. (That's not why we went, but as I admire my ostrich-clad feet, I must say it was a high point.) I have begun to feel like myself again. One awful moment: After the long flight, as the cab nears our building, I hear in my head as loudly as if he were saying it, Jon's voice exulting, "We're going to see a kitty!" just like he used to whenever we returned from a trip. (I hope he forgives me for revealing this.) My heart leaped in anticipation. Only he's not saying that, and we won't, ever again. I've lost my kitty. But then we go indoors, and I think I'll be okay.

On May 19, we adopt Musetta, a longhaired black-and-white female with an off-center star on her nose and round eyes like an owl's. She wasn't the only kitten at the Animal Rescue League that day, and we told each other that we didn't need to choose any yet. But then she reached out for us, little white mitten extended to draw our fingers close, and our hearts were hooked as well. She's got the loudest voice I've ever heard in a kitten, and when she peeps for attention she stares straight at you to make sure she's getting it. Just seven weeks old, she's not the most coordinated bundle of fur on the planet, and when she hops down the hallway she looks for all intents and purposes like a long-tailed bunny. She's not the old friend that Cyrus was, but she is adorable, and already she lets me stroke her belly. I see how trusting she is, and how soft. When she falls asleep next to me, purring like a little engine, I feel myself warm to her. This is, after all, a love story.

Acknowledgments

According to Rudyard Kipling, cats walk alone. Authors, however, don't, and there are plenty of people to thank for their help and support during the writing of this book. First and foremost, my gratitude goes to Peggy Leith Andersen, who first suggested I write about cats (even if she still doesn't want one) and to Debbie Jacobs for continued faith and encouragement. Thanks as well to my editor Dorsey Mills for relating, as well as editing, to my agent Colleen Mohyde, the estimable Rose Marie Morse of Morse Partners, and my adoptive editor Elizabeth Beier for professional skill and great heart. My fellow author and friend Vicki Croke early on shared data that helped me get started, and the sharp-eyed Karen Schlosberg and Brett Milano read and reread, much to my delight. All through the difficult period with Cyrus an additional crew came through, including Juli Kryslur, Leslie Greene, Anne Trumbore, Kris Fell, Cynthia Von Buhler, Louise Corrigan, Karen, Brett, and a score of others (including many of the folks previously mentioned). A general shout-out and hug, as well, to the women who consented to be interviewed about their own cats, many of whom shared sympathy and support with a distraught stranger who frequently was not at her best during interviews. Most of you are named in the text, a few of you under pseudonyms, and all of you helped me more than I can acknowledge. Dr. Melissa Clark made the ending as easy as possible, and Monique Ortiz of Boston's Animal Rescue League directed us toward Musetta, for which relief much thanks. And finally, of course, my thanks go to Jon Garelick, for his love as well as his careful editing. You make me purr.

Cat Rescue Organizations

These are just a sampling of the many groups around the world that help cats and other animals, including fortunate authors. Many of these have opportunities for volunteers, and most can use your donations as well.

Alley Cat Allies
1801 Belmont Road NW, Suite 201
Washington, DC 20009
www.alleycat.org

American Society for the Prevention of Cruelty to Animals
24 East 92nd Street
New York, NY 10128
www.aspca.org

Animal Rescue League of Boston
10 Chandler St.
Boston, MA 02117
www.arl-boston.org

Delta Society
289 Perimeter Road East
Renton, WA 98055
www.deltasociety.org

Friends of Plymouth Pound
P.O. Box 578
Manomet, MA. 02345
www.gis.net/~fpp

Massachusetts Society for the Prevention of Cruelty to Animals
350 South Huntington Avenue
Boston, MA 02130
www.mspca.org

SHAID (Shelter for Helpless Animals in Distress) Tree Animal
Shelter
950 Mullock Road, RR #3
Bridgewater, Nova Scotia, Canada B4V 2W2
SHAID@ns.sympatico.ca

Delmarva Cat Connection
PO Box 1818
Ocean City, MD 21842
www.mgrafix.com/towncats/towncats.html

Bibliography

Avanzino, Richard. "The Importance of Companion Animals to Society." Sydney, Australia: Australian Veterinary Association, 6 November 1996.

Baring, Anne, and Jules Cashford. *The Myth of the Goddess: Evolution of an Image*. New York: Viking, 1991.

Campbell, Joseph. *Primitive Mythology: The Masks of God*. New York: Viking, 1959.

Caras, Roger A. *A Celebration of Cats*. New York: Simon and Schuster, 1986.

Churcher, P. B., and J. H. Lawton. "Predation by Domestic Cats in an English Village." *The Journal of Zoology*, vol. 212. Cambridge University Press, London: 1987, 439–455.

Conway, D. J. *Animal Magic: The Art of Recognizing and Working with Familiars*. St. Paul, Minn: Llewellyn Publications, 2000.

Dekkers, Midas. *Dearest Pet: On Bestiality*. Trans. Paul Vincent. New York: Verso Books, 2000.

Dodman, Nicholas H. *The Cat Who Cried for Help: Attitudes, Emotions, and the Psychology of Cats*. New York: Bantam Doubleday Dell, 1999.

Eisler, Riane. *The Chalice and the Blade: Our History, Our Future*. New York: HarperCollins, 1987.

Fimrite, Peter, and Ray Delgado. "Cats Overrun Squalid Home in Petaluma." *San Francisco Chronicle* (24 May 2001).

Fox, Dr. Michael W. *Understanding Your Cat*. New York: St. Martin's Press, 1974.

Freeman, Lisa M., and Kathryn E. Michel. "Evaluation of Raw Food Diets for Dogs." *Journal of the American Veterinary Medical Association* 218, no. 5 (1 March 2001): 705–709.

Graham, Bernie. *Creature Comfort: Animals That Heal*. Amherst, N.Y.: Prometheus Books, 2000.

Hathaway, Nancy. *The Friendly Guide to Mythology*. New York: Viking-Penguin, 2001.

Hausman, Gerald, and Loretta Hausman. *The Mythology of Cats: Feline Legend and Lore Through the Ages*. New York: St. Martin's Press, 1997.

Hoarding of Animals Research Consortium, corresponding author Randy Frost, Ph.D. "People Who Hoard Animals." *Psychiatric Times* 4, vol. XVII (April 2000).

Horn, Stacy. *Waiting for My Cats to Die: A Morbid Memoir*. New York: St. Martin's Press, 2001.

Jampel, Barbara, writer and producer. *Cats: Caressing the Tiger*. Tim Kelly and Tom Simon, executive producers. A National Geographic Society Special, National Geographic Society and WQED, Pittsburgh, Penn., 1991.

Johnson-Bennett, Pam. *Hiss and Tell*. New York: Penguin Books, 1994.

Jung, Carl G. *The Archetypes and the Collective Unconscious* 2nd ed., translated by R.F.C. Hull. Princeton, N.J.: Princeton University Press, 1969.

MacDonough, Katharine. *Reigning Cats and Dogs: A History of Pets at Court Since the Renaissance*. New York: St. Martin's Press, 1999.

Marquis, Don. *Archy and Mehitabel*. New York: Anchor Books, 1990.

National Pet Owners Survey, 2001–2002. Greenwich, Conn.: American Pet Products Manufacturers Association, 2001.

Pet Owner Survey, 1998. Denver, Colo.: American Animal Hospital Association, 1998.

"Pets Can Tame High Blood Pressure." Atlanta, Ga.: American Heart Association (abstract 174), 7 November 1999.

Pollack, Andrew. "Cloning a Cat to End the Sniffing and Sneezing of Its Owner." *The New York Times* (27 June 2001): C1.

Robbins, Trina. *The Great Women Superheroes*, Northampton, Mass.: Kitchen Sink Press, 1996.

Saunders, Nicholas J. *Animal Spirits: An Illustrated Guide*. Boston: Little Brown, 1995.

——. *The Cult of the Cat*. London: Thames and Hudson, 1991.

Schultz, Stacey. "Pets and their Humans." *U.S. News & World Report* 17, vol. 129 (30 October 2000): 53–55.

Spadafori, Gina, and Paul D. Pion DVM, DACVM. *Cats for Dummies*. Foster City, Calif.: IDG Books, 1997.

Taylor, David. *The Ultimate Cat Book*. New York: Simon and Schuster, 1989.

Thomas, Elizabeth Marshall. *The Tribe of Tiger: Cats and Their Cultures*. New York: Simon and Schuster, 1994.

"U.S. Pet Ownership and Demographic Sourcebook." Schaumberg, Ill.: American Veterinary Medical Association, 1997.

Whyte, Malcolm. *Great Comic Cats*. San Francisco: Pomegranate Press, 2001.